film

film

isms... UNDERSTANDING CINEMA

RONALD BERGAN

UNIVERSE

Contents

THE FIRST SOUND DECADE
1928–38

Hollywood Studioism
36

Horrorism
40

Surrealism
42

Gangsterism
44

Screwballism
48

Exoticism
50

Escapism
52

Cartoonism
54

Poetic Realism
56

Costume Romanticism
58

Anti-Militarism
62

THE WAR YEARS
1939–45

Propagandism
66

Socialist Realism
68

Racialism
70

Naturalism
72

Realism
74

Film Noirism
76

Emotionalism
78

Biographism
80

THE POST-WAR ERA
1946–59

Italian Neo-Realism
86

Utopianism
88

Westernism
92

Musicalism
94

Orientalism
98

Experimentalism
100

Liberalism
102

Classicism
104

Teenagism
106

THE SIXTIES AND BEYOND
1960–

New Wavism
110

Auteurism
112

Eroticism
116

Dystopianism
118

Revisionism
120

American Indianism
122

Postmodernism
124

Dogmatism
128

Disasterism
130

Cultism
132

Minimalism
136

Asian Minimalism
138

Feminism
138

Porn
140

REFERENCE SECTION

Introduction
6

How to use
this book
8

Chronology
of Isms
144

Glossary
of useful terms
148

Glossary
of Names
148

Glossary
of Films
154

Credits
159

Introduction

This book is a guide through the various movements, trends, terms and social and historical contexts which make up the history of film. Although there are many ways of understanding 'the seventh art', this book approaches cinema through the prism of shared systems of beliefs, attitudes and aesthetics. Unlike the other arts, most films are primarily defined by genres rather than isms, but this book, while admitting the dominance of genre, provides a wider perspective.

First, one must accept that, despite films being made collectively, it is the director who is considered the principal creator of the film. This is straightforward when considering the work of auteurs, many of whom contribute to the screenplays, often edit, even photograph their films and have the say on the final cut. Nevertheless, those directors in the Hollywood mainstream who have to satisfy so many different people – the moneymen, the producer, the distributors etc – still have their names attached to the title of the film. This is clarified in the chapter on auteurism, in which will be found certain auteurs who are so original or individual that they do not fit conveniently into any ism. On the other hand, there are directors and films that belong to more than one ism.

It should be remembered that isms are not always hard and fast categories and in each ism there are sometimes developments, changes and disagreements which can constitute considerable differences between directors and films gathered under one ism. But a pattern emerges of what links certain isms and what separates them.

No definition of an ism can be final. Some stay within fixed parameters, others are more fluid. It should also be stressed that examining films from what could be called,

an 'ismatic' viewpoint has necessitated the coining of new isms like screwballism and horrorism, but most of them are bona fide.

Despite the fact that a majority of isms have existed throughout the comparatively short history of cinema, certain eras are more apposite than others in which to place them. For example, even though the western dates from the early silent days, and that one of the first to gain artistic status was John Ford's *Stagecoach* (1939), westernism is placed in the Post-War Era section because its golden age stretched from 1946–56. It is necessary to bear in mind this logic when the dates of some key works are outside the time period of the section.

Because films are made throughout the world in different languages, decisions have to be made about titles in a language other than English. In general, the English titles are given. Sometimes both the original and English titles are used, when the film is known by both titles. When only the original title is given, it means that the film was released and known only under that title.

Although the book attempts to be as inclusive as possible, it does not pretend to be a comprehensive history of cinema, nor a 100-best listing. If the reader does not find a favourite film here, then it might be instructive and amusing to try attaching the film to an appropriate ism or isms, after becoming familiar with the 51 examples that follow.

THE FOUR TYPES OF ISM

1 GENRE RELATED
eg westernism, gangsterism

The concept of genres was established at the beginning of the period of the Hollywood studio system. It helped production decisions and made films easier to market. When studios were turning out films at a rapid rate, the generic concept provided scriptwriters with a template on which to work. When a film is labelled a western, a musical or a film noir, audiences already have certain preconceptions about what genre or kind of film it is. Although films differ in many respects, in each category, all the genre-related isms share recognisable patterns in terms of theme, period and plot, and their use of iconography and the type of characters portrayed.

2 SUB-GENRE RELATED
eg screwballism, teenagism

Sub-genres exist under the wider umbrella of a major genre, but have their own distinctive subject matter, style and iconography. Screwballism and slapstickism are obviously sub-genres of comedy, whereas, although teenagism could also be classed as a sub-genre of comedy, it could also be a branch of the musical or horror. Emotionalism, eroticism and exoticism set up certain self-explanatory expectations, while feminism, racialism and anti-militarism are sub-genres solely in their approach to subject matter.

3 ARTISTIC MOVEMENTS
eg expressionism, surrealism

Cinema is not isolated from the other arts. In fact, Sergei Eisenstein claimed that cinema was a 'synthesis of all the arts'. Although film has a specificity, it has been influenced to some extent by other 20th-century artistic movements. For example, German expressionist films and surrealist French films were created in parallel to expressionism and surrealism in the other arts in the 1920s. More recently, postmodernism and minimalism have applied equally to films as to music and architecture.

4 SPECIFIC PERIODS
eg constructivism, Italian neo-realism

Although most isms stretch over long periods, with highs and lows, some isms only flourished during specific short periods with which they are immediately associated, rather like fauvism and cubism in painting. In the Soviet Union, constructivism gave way to its antithesis, socialist realism, each ism set in the political climate of the day. Likewise poetic realism in France in the 1930s and Italian neo-realism in the 1940s.

How to use this book

GR Symbols are used throughout the book to distinguish between the four types of ism outlined in the introduction. This means you can tell at a glance whether an ism is genre related **GR**, sub-genre related **SGR**, an artistic movement **AM** or a specific period **SP**.

INTRODUCTION
The first section offers a brief introduction to the ism, giving a succinct summary of its main features.

KEY NAMES
This is a list of the most important directors, and in a few instances actors, producers and screenwriters, related to the ism. Exploring the films of such key directors would give a comprehensive knowledge of and feeling for the ism.

KEY WORDS
These sum up the key concepts, styles or issues relating to the ism and provide a map of associations that will help you to quickly chart an ism, and enable easier recollection of it.

MAIN DEFINITION
This explores the ism in more depth than the brief introduction, explaining the significance of the ism, its history and ideas, and the methods and stylistic features which distinguish it from, or relate it to, other isms.

When a movie is labelled a western, a musical, a film noir or a romantic comedy, preconceptions and expectations are automatically raised with audiences. Revisionist cinema reinterprets, challenges or even satirises traditional genres.

SAM PECKINPAH 1925–84; ROBERT ALTMAN 1925–2006; SERGIO LEONE 1929–89; CLINT EASTWOOD 1930–; RAINER WERNER FASSBINDER 1946–82; PEDRO ALMODÓVAR 1949– ; JIM JARMUSCH 1953– ; JOEL COEN 1955– ; ETHAN COEN 1957–

anti-Establishment; cynical; demythological; self-reflexive

In Marxist politics, revisionism meant a move away from a revolutionary position to an evolutionary or reformist one. In the same way, revisionist films do not take a revolutionary stand against an accepted genre, but simply question its longstanding assumptions and make changes within it. Revisionist films, which derive from an affection and feeling for the genre, tend to be self-reflexive and self-conscious. In the more liberal 1960s, emerging filmmakers used the basic tenets of genre films for their own purposes, such as to expand their criticism of conservative values in society. The revisionist impulse appeared when myth had seemed to have overtaken reality, necessitating a reminder of forgotten principles.

The first films of the French New Wave directors were not immediately recognisable as 'art cinema'. François Truffaut, in his second feature, moved into gangster territory with *Shoot the Pianist* (1960), based on a David Goodis thriller. Jean-Luc Godard with *Breathless* (1959), dedicated to Monogram Pictures (the all-B movie studio), attempted to recapture (and comment on) the directness and economy of the American gangster movie. With *Une femme*

est une femme (A Woman is a Woman), 1961), Godard paid homage to the MGM musical and, in *Alphaville* (1965), he used the trappings of pulp fiction and film noir to tell a futuristic story.

Revisionist war films sought to desimplify attitudes to military conflict. Revisionist melodramas, of which Rainer Werner Fassbinder and Pedro Almodóvar were masters, unpicked the moral restrictions on them. The revisionist western generally favoured an anti-hero (often unglamorous and crude), stronger roles for women, and more sympathetic portrayals of both native and African Americans, and tended to be more violent and realistic. Sam Peckinpah's westerns like *Ride the High Country* (1962) and *The Wild Bunch* (1969) showed old-time cowboys ill at ease with the new-style West.

The Italian Sergio Leone, who took on the sacrosanct American genre of the western, branded it with his own style of amoral mythic grandeur. Clint Eastwood, who appeared in three Leone westerns, brought many of the revisionist elements of the spaghetti western into his own films as

director, which demythologised the conventions of earlier westerns. Meanwhile, Czechoslovakia and East Germany lampooned the western from an Eastern European Communist perspective in *Lemonade Joe* (1964) and *Sons of the Great Bear* (1966) respectively.

Film noir, which already takes a bleak view of human nature, seemed less open to revisionism, but loosening constraints on sex and violence gave directors such as Robert Altman (*The Long Goodbye*, 1973), Roman Polanski (*Chinatown*, 1974), Curtis Hanson *LA Confidential* (1997) and the Coen Brothers in many of their films starting with *Blood Simple* (1984) a chance to further explore the genre in neo-noirs.

KEY WORKS
* The Good, the Bad and the Ugly, 1966, SERGIO LEONE
Despite the film's title, none of the characters is good, though Clint Eastwood is bad and handsome as the monosyllabic, super-cool, poncho-clad, cheroot chomping bounty hunter nicknamed 'Blondie'. With the stylised violence, the circular tracking shots, long silent close-ups, meaningful pauses and looks, Leone has attempted to create the apotheosis of the western.

↓ Chinatown, 1974, ROMAN POLANSKI
In 1930s Los Angeles, Jack Nicholson as a Chandleresque private eye investigates a murky crime involving a corrupt tycoon and his daughter. In fact, Nicholson spends most of the movie with a white plaster on his nose as a result of a knifing by a nasty little hoodlum played by Polanski himself

OTHER WORKS
Breathless (À bout de souffle), 1959, GODARD; Shoot the Pianist, 1960, TRUFFAUT; Une femme est une femme (A Woman is a Woman), 1961, GODARD; Ride the High Country, 1962, PECKINPAH; Lemonade Joe, 1964, LIPSKÝ; Alphaville, 1965, GODARD; Sons of the Great Bear, 1966, MACH; The Wild Bunch, 1969, PECKINPAH; Little Big Man, 1970, PENN; M*A*S*H, 1970, ALTMAN; The Bitter Tears of Petra Von Kant, 1972, FASSBINDER; The Long Goodbye, 1973, ALTMAN; Blood Simple, 1984, COEN; LA Confidential, 1997, HANSON; All About My Mother, 1999, ALMODÓVAR; The Man Who Wasn't There, 2001, COEN

Anti-Militarism; Liberalism; New Wavism; Postmodernism; Feminism

Propagandism; Socialist Realism; Racialism; Classicism; Utopianism

KEY WORKS

Each ism is illustrated by two (sometimes three) works. These have been chosen because they best exemplify the features of the ism that are discussed in the Introduction, Key Words and Main Definition.

OTHER WORKS

This list is a supplement to the Key Works. All are good examples of the ism they have been chosen to illustrate.

SEE ALSO

 Isms are often interrelated. Those listed under See Also share ideas and styles with the ism under discussion.

DON'T SEE

 Isms are also antithetical to each other, or predicated on mutually exclusive, and incompatible, assumptions, methods or ideas. The isms listed under Don't See are in some way out of tune with the ism being discussed.

Other resources included in this book

CHRONOLOGY OF ISMS

This time line shows the lifespan of all the isms included in the book. However, unlike isms in the other arts, most of those in cinema, less than 120 years old, run from the very early days until the present. Nevertheless, each has peak periods or a golden age, which is clearly indicated. The time line therefore shows an approximation of the most creative and productive period of the ism, even though there are excellent representatives outside of that period. The prime examples of this are westernism and musicalism, the former making an early

appearance at the beginning of the 20th century, the latter created at the coming of sound, but both of which are now almost extinct.

GLOSSARY OF USEFUL TERMS

This contains a general selection of mostly technical terms that have been used in the definitions of the isms.

GLOSSARY OF NAMES

Directors and actors who have been identified as Key Names in the chapters are gathered in this alphabetical list for easy reference. The list also includes dates of birth and death, as well as the ism or isms with which the figures are most closely identified.

GLOSSARY OF FILMS

An easy-reference alphabetical listing of the films mentioned in the Key Works and Other Works sections for each ism.

THE SILENT ERA
1895–1927

◐ Illusionism in films makes no claims to represent reality. In fact, it draws attention to its flight from realism, often with the aid of special effects. Like magicians, illusionist directors delight in trickery, intentionally asking audiences *not* to suspend their disbelief.

◓ **GEORGES MÉLIÈS** 1861–1938; **JEAN COCTEAU** 1889–1963; **BUSBY BERKELEY** 1895–1976; **JAN ŠVANKMAJER** 1934–; **TERRY GILLIAM** 1940–; **TIM BURTON** 1958–

◑ animation; fantasy; special effects; trick photography

● It can be argued that most films are in some respect fantasies because they produce illusions by the manipulation of a filmed event using various forms of cinematographic and montage effects. But illusionist films emphasise the cinema's ability to realise alternative spatio-temporal frameworks and 'impossible' experiences. Magic counterbalancing what is perceived to be the sterility of rationalism is the essence of illusionism in films.

Early cinema was fascinated by its own fantastic subversion of the physical laws of space-time and causality to which spectators were subjugated. It immediately recognised the medium's inherent illusionism, first in plotless displays of

cinematic magic, then in narratives in which the characters were drawn into the fantasy.

Not long after the birth of cinema, two distinctive paths were taken: the films of the Lumière brothers, which attempted to capture reality, and those of Georges Méliès, which did everything to deflect from it. Méliès – conjurer, cartoonist, inventor and mechanic – experimented with trick photography to create magical effects. He went on to develop many devices such as superimposition, multiple exposure, matting, the dissolve, and stop motion. For example, in *The Melomaniac* (1903), Méliès plays a music master who removes his head only for it to be replaced by another, and another. As the music master throws each head onto a telegraph wire, they form a series of musical notes. *A Trip to the Moon (Le voyage dans la lune*, 1902) enacts the transformation of the cinema into an impossible world in which the spaceship crashes into the eye of the Man on the Moon.

Méliès' example was followed by a great many illusionist films that took their inspiration from Arabian Nights tales to fairy stories to *Harry Potter*. Raoul Walsh's *The Thief of Bagdad* (1924) set new Hollywood standards for special effects, enabling Douglas Fairbanks to climb up a magic rope, ride a winged horse and sail over the rooftops on a magic carpet.

The Wizard of Oz (1939) makes the distinction between reality and fantasy by showing Dorothy's dream domain in glorious Technicolor and her home in Kansas in dull monochrome. Yet the message of the film is 'There's no place like home', because the country of Oz is depicted as an illusion and the Wizard turns out to be a charlatan.

Some directors who started as animators, like Tim Burton, Terry Gilliam and Jan Švankmajer, often combined animation with

↑ Beauty and the Beast (La belle et la bête), 1945,
JEAN COCTEAU
Jean Cocteau's favourite actor, Jean Marais, as the
Beast, in his extraordinary feline make-up (by Hagop
Arakelian), wines and dines Beauty (Josette Day) but
does not wish to show her his face. The candelabra on
the table is held by a human hand, part of the magical
environment imagined by Jean Cocteau and realised by
production designer Christian Bérard.

live action, or saw live action in terms of
animation. Busby Berkeley, however, was a
stage choreographer who created his
kaleidoscopic, art deco and trompe l'oeil
effects with high overhead shots from a
mobile crane or dollying in on lines of
identically dressed chorus girls.

Although Jean Cocteau was allied to the
surrealists, his *Beauty and the Beast* (*La belle
et la bête*, 1945) uses tricks to enchant
rather than to shock.

KEY WORKS

← A Trip to The Moon (Le voyage dans la lune), 1902,
GEORGES MÉLIÈS
One of the most famous and earliest images of
illusionism in the cinema foresaw animation. George
Méliès brought his own vision on this adaptation of
Jules Verne's futuristic novel, with a real grimacing face
superimposed on a drawing for the Man in The Moon,
struck in the eye by a spaceship.

OTHER WORKS

The Melomaniac, 1903, MÉLIÈS; The Thief of Bagdad,
1924, WALSH; The Wizard of Oz, 1939, FLEMING;
Münchausen, 1943, VON BÁKY; The Saragossa
Manuscript, 1964, HAS; Time Bandits, 1981, GILLIAM;
Alice, 1988, ŠVANKMAJER; Charlie and the Chocolate
Factory, 2005, BURTON

 Expressionism; Surrealism; Cartoonism;
Escapism; FX-ism

 Socialist Realism; Naturalism; Realism; Film
Noirism; Minimalism

🕐 Madcap chases, pratfalls and pies in the face are the elements most associated with slapstick comedy, but the term is used more widely to cover all silent film physical comedy, including that of Charlie Chaplin, Buster Keaton, Harold Lloyd and Harry Langdon, who took it to a higher level of sophistication.

🕐 **MACK SENNETT** 1880–1960; **MAX LINDER** 1883–1925; **ROSCOE 'FATTY' ARBUCKLE** 1887–1933; **CHARLIE CHAPLIN** 1889–1977; **STAN LAUREL** 1890–1965; **OLIVER HARDY** 1892–1957; **HAL ROACH** 1892–1992; **HAROLD LLOYD** 1893–1971; **HARRY LANGDON** 1894–1944; **BUSTER KEATON** 1895–1966

🕐 athletic stunts; car chases; custard pies; pratfalls, speeded-up action

🕐 Slapstick derived its name from the wooden sticks that circus clowns slapped together to prompt audience applause, but has come to mean most visual comedy that does not depend on sound to be effective. The very first example in the history of cinema was in 1895: the Lumière brothers' *Watering the Gardener*, which depicts a gardener receiving a jet of water in his face when a naughty boy steps on a hose and then releases it.

Most of the earliest comedies were made by the French, and in 1907 the Pathé company launched a series of shorts featuring André Deed, cinema's first true comic star. The most gifted and influential film comedian was Max Linder from France whom Charlie Chaplin acknowledged as 'the Professor to whom I owe everything'. While the other comic stars were manic and grotesque, Linder adopted the character of a bemused dandy with sleek hair, trimmed moustache, and a silk hat that survived all catastrophes.

It was not until 1912 that American film comedy emerged with Mack Sennett for the Keystone Company and the Keystone Kops, the bumbling group of policemen that supported many of the silent comics. Using speeded-up action, reverse motion and other camera and editing tricks, Sennett established the type of rapid irreverent

comedy forever associated with his name. The films usually ended with a chase of death-defying thrills with many stunts executed by the comedians themselves. Sennett filmed the throwing of the first custard pie, by Mabel Normand at Roscoe

KEY WORKS

↓ **City Lights,** 1931, CHARLIE CHAPLIN
In his iconic guise as the Little Tramp, Chaplin, using his last cent, buys a flower from a blind girl (Virginia Cherrill) who believes him to be a millionaire. Although the film was made four years after talkies, Chaplin preferred to use only sound effects and music to keep his vast international audience.

'Fatty' Arbuckle, in *A Noise from the Deep* (1913) and also made the first feature-length American comedy, *Tilly's Punctured Romance* (1914), which starred Marie Dressler and Chaplin. Sennett's rival was Hal Roach, whose studio had Harold Lloyd, the Our Gang kids, and Stan Laurel and Oliver Hardy under contract.

The four giants of American silent film comedy – Chaplin, Keaton, Lloyd and Langdon – all emerged from one- or two-reelers to make features in the 1920s. Chaplin first broke away from the mechanical and crude techniques of the Sennett comedies and introduced pathos and a detailed social background into his

more structured and ambitious farces, *City Lights* (1931) being the best example. Keaton's films were supreme examples of visual comedy allied to cinematic technique, the multitude of gags depending on cutting, camera setups and spacio-temporal tensions. This reached its peak in *The General* (1926). Langdon cultivated the

character of what the writer and critic James Agee called 'an elderly baby'. Lloyd introduced a comedy of thrills by hanging precariously on the side of a skyscraper. Despite being best known for these feats, of the 300 films Lloyd made, only five contain such sequences.

Although the coming of sound diminished slapstick comedy, the tradition of sight gags was continued, notably by Laurel and Hardy, and later by popular teams such as Bud Abbott and Lou Costello, and Dean Martin and Jerry Lewis. Peter Sellers fell about as the maladroit Inspector Clouseau in the *Pink Panther* series, while Jacques Tati and Pierre Étaix, in France, and Toto, in Italy, kept visual comedy alive. In 1963, Stanley Kramer paid a mammoth three-hour tribute to slapstickism with *It's a Mad, Mad, Mad, Mad World*.

← **The General,** 1926, CLYDE BRUCKMAN / BUSTER KEATON
The film, shot on location, is distinctive for its American Civil War setting, with the cinematography reminiscent of Mathew B. Brady's contemporary photographs. Buster Keaton makes much comic play with mechanical objects such as a capricious canon and the eponymous locomotive he drives.

OTHER WORKS
Watering the Gardener, 1895, LUMIÈRE BROTHERS; **A Noise from the Deep,** 1913, SENNETT; **Tilly's Punctured Romance,** 1914, SENNETT; **The Three Must-Get-Theirs,** 1922, LINDER; **Safety Last,** 1923, NEWMEYER/TAYLOR; **Long Pants,** 1927, CAPRA; **Steamboat Bill, Jr,** 1928, REISNER / KEATON; **The Music Box,** 1932, PARROTT; **It's a Mad, Mad, Mad, Mad World,** 1963, KRAMER

 Athleticism; Hollywood Studioism; Surrealism; Screwballism; Escapism

 Socialist Realism; Film Noirism; Emotionalism; Italian Neo-Realism; Minimalism

Narratives in the monumentalist tradition surpass the ordinary in scale. The films are usually made on a very large budget, feature vast panoramas with hundreds of extras, follow the adventures of a legendary hero and are likely to be biblical or historical stories.

MARIO CASERINI 1874–1920; DW GRIFFITH 1875–1948; CECIL B DEMILLE 1881–1959; GIOVANNI PASTRONE 1883–1959; ANTHONY MANN 1906–94; NICHOLAS RAY 1911–79

big budgets; crowd scenes; historical subjects; large casts and sets; pageantry; wide vistas

Films on a monumental or epic scale are dependent on large budgets because of the elaborate period settings, on-location shooting, huge casts and episodic structure. There is, however, a perception that many of them tend to be over-inflated and too extravagant, offering exciting and spectacular action at the expense of characterisation.

The 'historical-mythological' genre was born in Italy in the early part of the 20th century. The films, many of which were set in ancient Rome, were intended to inspire patriotism and religious values as much as to entertain. Enrico Guazzoni's *Quo Vadis?* (1912) was, at over two hours' running time, the longest film ever presented in the US. This was followed by Mario Caserini's *The Last Days of Pompei* (1913). However, the most influential and most successful of the early Italian epics was Giovanni Pastrone's *Cabiria* (1914).

One of the most expensive films to date, *Cabiria* was a huge spectacle about the adventures of a slave girl and Maciste, her strong man companion and protector, during the Second Punic War. (Maciste, and variants such as Hercules, later became the heroes of Italian *peplum,* or 'sword and sandal', movies.) The film's intertitles, which were written by Gabriele d'Annunzio, the most famous Italian writer of the day, gave it cultural credibility, allowing it to become the first film that merited a complete review in the Italian press.

As a result of the Italian epics, the other major filmmaking countries increased their output of grandiose productions. In America DW Griffith was inspired to embark on his large-scale productions, the first being the four-reel biblical spectacle *Judith of Bethulia* (1914), which marked American cinema's transition from shorts to features. His *Intolerance* (1916) is directly influenced by the Italian epics, though it is more original in form. It contains four separate stories to illustrate the theme of the title: a modern story, the crucifixion, the massacre of the Protestants in Paris in 1572, and the fall of Babylon.

Cecil B DeMille is mostly associated with grandiose productions, starting with *The Ten Commandments* (1923), which he remade over three decades later with even more resources at his disposal. Fred Niblo's *Ben-Hur: A Tale of the Christ* (1925), which contained a huge sea battle and a breathtaking chariot race, was also remade even more spectacularly in the 1950s. The introduction of widescreen processes – the first in CinemaScope was Henry Koster's *The Robe* (1953) – often dictated the content of the movies. Therefore Richard Thorpe's *Knights of the Round Table* (1953), Howard Hawks' *Land of the Pharaohs* (1955) and Robert Wise's *Helen of Troy* (1956) and others filled the screens. In the 1960s, in the latter part of their careers, Anthony Mann and Nicholas Ray made impressive excursions into the genre with huge Samuel

Bronston productions shot in Spain, the best being Mann's *El Cid* (1961). The relative failure of the $40 million *Cleopatra* (Joseph L Mankiewicz, 1963) put a brake on monumentalism, which has since resurfaced only rarely over the years, examples being Ridley Scott's *Gladiator* (2000) and *Robin Hood* (2010) and Wolfgang Petersen's *Troy* (2004)

KEY WORKS

← **The Ten Commandments,** 1956, CECIL B DEMILLE
Charlton Heston as Moses returns from Mount Sinai with God's new 'thou shalt not' laws for man. Heston was made up to bear a resemblance to Michelangelo's statue of Moses in Rome. The film, DeMille's last, was his only one in a widescreen process, VistaVision in this case.

→ **Intolerance,** 1916, DW GRIFFITH
Griffith conceived the largest movie backdrop ever created until then for the Belshazzar's Feast sequence. The set has Egyptian bas-reliefs, Hindu elephant gods, and Assyrian bulls, a mixture of Near Eastern styles represented on the walls and in the costumes. The staging and art direction were largely inspired by the grandiose works of Victorian painter Lawrence Alma-Tadema.

OTHER WORKS

The Last Days of Pompeii, 1913, CASERINI; **Cabiria,** 1914, PASTRONE; **Judith of Bethulia,** 1914, DW GRIFFITH; **Ben-Hur: A Tale of the Christ,** 1925, NIBLO; **Knights of the Round Table,** 1953, THORPE; **The Robe,** 1953, KOSTER; **Land of the Pharaohs,** 1955, HAWKS; **Helen of Troy,** 1956, WISE; **Quo Vadis?,** 1956, LEROY; **Ben Hur,** 1959, WYLER; **El Cid,** 1961, MANN; **Cleopatra,** 1963, MANKIEWICZ; **Gladiator,** 2000, RIDLEY SCOTT; **Troy,** 2004, PETERSEN

Hollywood Studioism; Exoticism; Escapism; Disasterism

Avant-Gardism; Italian Neo-Realism; American Indieism; Dogmetism; Minimalism

Athleticism leaps across various movie genres such as action thrillers, swashbuckling period pieces, martial arts films and sports-related pictures, but the raison d'être of all of them is their focus on the physical prowess of the hero or heroine.

DOUGLAS FAIRBANKS 1883–1939; ERROL FLYNN 1909–59; BURT LANCASTER 1913–94; JEAN MARAIS 1913–98; TOSHIRO MIFUNE 1920–97; PHILIPPE DE BROCA 1933–2004; JEAN-PAUL BELMONDO 1933–; BRUCE LEE 1940–73; JACKIE CHAN 1954–; ANG LEE 1954–

action; constant movement; full body framing; heroism

Part of the specificity of the cinema is its ability to follow an actor in time and space. If the actor is a naturally gifted athlete then all the better for action scenes in which the use of stunt artists or special effects can be limited. Regardless of the genre, the overriding athleticism of the star determines that the plot revolves around his or her physical prowess, which helps overcome their enemies.

Athletic protagonists were particularly abundant in silent cinema, where body language had to substitute for dialogue. Douglas Fairbanks believed that movies were about movement, and his films were built around his muscular athleticism. Whether diving off ocean liners, vaulting through the glades of Sherwood Forest or sliding down the sails of a Spanish galleon, he was almost always in perpetual motion.

The Mark of Zorro (1920) launched Fairbanks as a swashbuckler, and he continued to flash his sword in *The Three Musketeers* (1921) and *Robin Hood* (1922) among others. These set the pattern for his worthy successors in the US such as Errol Flynn, Tyrone Power, Stewart Granger and Burt Lancaster. The latter, who exulted in physical action, out-leaped and out-swashbuckled his predecessors in *The Flame and the Arrow* (1950) and *The Crimson Pirate* (1952), acrobatic spoofs for which Lancaster's circus experience came in handy. Jean Marais and Jean-Paul Belmondo (mainly in the films of Philippe de Broca)

carried on the tradition in France. In Japan, Toshiro Mifune's dynamic physicality dominated many a samurai movie.

Martial-arts films, simple affairs of good versus evil, include a series of brilliantly choreographed fights in which the hero is outnumbered by his enemies, who are armed with knives or clubs, but defeats them with his bare hands and feet. Bruce Lee, above all, was responsible for the popularity of the genre, his short career culminating with *Enter the Dragon* (1973). Director-actor Jackie Chan combined slapstick comedy with high-energy action, performing all his own stunts, often at his own peril.

Chan, dubbed 'the Buster Keaton of Kung Fu', was an admirer of the sight gags and pratfalls of many silent-film comics, particularly Keaton and Harold Lloyd. In the climax of *College* (1927), Keaton executes a series of athletic feats in order to rescue his girlfriend from a bully.

Sports movies, by definition, focus on athletic achievement and have similar plot lines. We see the sportspeople's home life, training, struggles, blood, sweat and tears, whereas their opponents are impersonal machines, or the bad guys to be defeated or an obstacle to be overcome on the road to self-esteem. More films have been made about boxing than any other sport because it is easier to frame two people in conflict on the screen than it is to capture the sometimes complex pattern of a team game. It provides a clear-cut, one-to-one dramatic situation.

KEY WORKS

← The Adventures of Robin Hood, 1938, MICHAEL CURTIZ, WILLIAM KEIGHLEY
Errol Flynn (right), in the title role, has a climactic battle with Basil Rathbone as his nemesis Sir Guy of Gisbourne, both actors being skilled swordsmen. A model of the swashbuckling genre, it was the first in three-strip Technicolor, thus contrasting the forest greens of Robin Hood's Merry Men and the deep reds of John's court.

↑ Enter the Dragon, 1973, ROBERT CLOUSE,
Bruce Lee displays his lethal kicks against the evil Han (Shih Kien). Before computer-generated imagery made much of the action defy the laws of gravity and physics, Lee's fights had the excitement of authenticity. This was his last completed film before his mysterious death at the age of 32.

OTHER WORKS

The Mark of Zorro, 1920, NIBLO; The Three Musketeers, 1921, NIBLO; Robin Hood, 1922, DWAN; The Thief of Bagdad, 1924, WALSH; College, 1927, HORNE / KEATON; The Flame and the Arrow, 1950, TOURNEUR; The Crimson Pirate, 1952, SIODMAK; Raging Bull, 1980, SCORSESE; Crouching Tiger, Hidden Dragon, 2000, ANG LEE; Hero, 2002, YIMOU; Kung Fu Hustle, 2004, CHOW

 Slapstickism; Escapism; Utopianism; Westernism; Musicalism

 Poetic Realism; Film Noirism; Auterism; Minimalism; Asian Minimalism; FX-ism

With its stylised, distorted sets, grotesquely angled photography and artificial lighting creating a nightmarish atmosphere, Robert Wiene's *The Cabinet of Dr Caligari* (1919) became a trademark of German cinema in the 1920s. The style was too rarefied to have been much imitated though it inspired a number of horror fantasies, or 'shadow films'.

ROBERT WIENE 1873–1938; PAUL WEGENER 1874–1948; PAUL LENI 1885–1929; FW MURNAU 1889–1931; JAMES WHALE 1889–1957; FRITZ LANG 1890–1976

artificiality; distortion; dream-like atmosphere; menace; shadows

Caligari (Werner Krauss), a weird-looking, bespectacled fairground showman, presents to the public a somnambulist Cesare (Conrad Veidt), who answers questions about the future. In the meantime, Caligari hypnotises Cesare, who sleeps in a coffin-like box, to carry off the girlfriend (Lil Dagover) of the young hero (Friedrich Feher) and commit murder.

The original screenplay of *The Cabinet of Dr Caligari* by Carl Mayer and Hans Janowitz (1919) was intended as a metaphor of the First World War, in which Caligari represented a government that hypnotised its people into sleepwalking into war. However, the ending shows Caligari as a benign director of a lunatic asylum, with the hero a patient who has imagined the whole eerie story.

The German sociologist Siegfried Kracauer, in *From Caligari to Hitler* (1947), an influential study of German cinema from 1919 to 1933, felt that by representing its story as a tale told by a madman, *The Cabinet of Dr Caligari* helped prepare the rise of Hitler by subtly diverting the audience from a serious appraisal of social realities:

'While the original story helped expose the madness inherent in authority, *Caligari* glorified it, and convicted its antagonist as mad. A revolutionary film was thus turned into a conformist one.'

But it provided Fritz Lang, who was originally assigned to direct *Caligari*, with the impetus to make *Dr Mabuse, The Gambler* (1922). This film, about a master criminal who builds an underworld empire with the intension of taking over the world, took the character of Caligari further, even foreshadowing Hitler.

Although considered to be the first true example of expressionism in the cinema, *Caligari* differs from many other

KEY WORKS
↳ **The Cabinet of Dr Caligari,** 1919, ROBERT WIENE
The somnabulist Cesare (Conrad Veidt), watched by the evil Dr Caligari (Werner Krauss), who has hypnotised him to carry off Jane Olsen (Lil Dagover), lays down his burden. Although much of the film is set in a fairground, the distorted painted decor by Walter Röhrig, Hermann Warm and Walter Reimann gives the whole film a feeling of nightmarish unreality.

↑ **Waxworks,** 1924, PAUL LENI
A young poet (future director Wilhelm Dieterle) in a fairground wax museum dreams of himself in stories involving three of the exhibits – the Caliph of Bagdad, Ivan the Terrible and Jack the Ripper. 'All the film seeks to engender is an indescribable fluidity of light, moving shapes, shadows, lines, and curves,' wrote Paul Leni.

OTHER WORKS
The Golem, 1920, WEGENER/BOESE; **Dr Mabuse,
The Gambler,** 1922, LANG ; Nosferatu, 1922, MURNAU;
Frankenstein, 1931, WHALE; **M,** 1931, FRITZ LANG;
The Bride of Frankenstein, 1935, WHALE;
Edward Scissorhands, 1990, BURTON

expressionist dramas because it stresses artificiality, all of it taking place within a studio, against painted theatrical sets with oblique lines and angles without perspective. The tone of the decor extends to the costumes and make-up that is heavily applied to the actors in the manner of circus or 'low farce' performers. The tall, gaunt Conrad Veidt's beautifully mimed expressionistic portrayal made him an international star. Among the few films that could be directly influenced by Caligari was Paul Leni's *Waxworks* (1924).

Perhaps the film's greatest indirect influence was on the horror films made in Hollywood at Universal Studios in the 1930s, particularly James Whale's *Frankenstein* (1931) and *The Bride of Frankenstein* (1935). *Caligari* was also a direct inspiration on Tim Burton, who modelled Johnny Depp's looks in *Edward Scissorhands* (1990) on those of the somnambulist played by Veidt.

 Expressionism; Avant-Gardism; Horrorism;
Film Noirism

 Realism; Italian Neo-Realism; Costume
Romanticism; Classicism; Utopianism

Expressionism, born in Germany out of the pessimism following the First World War, included theatre, architecture, music, painting and films. The highly stylised, atmospheric and symbolic films later influenced horror movies and film noir.

TOD BROWNING 1880–1962; GW PABST 1885–1967; FW MURNAU 1889–1931; FRITZ LANG 1890–1976; KARL FREUND 1890–1969; EA DUPONT 1891–1956

chiaroscuro; distortion; fatalism; Freudianism; oblique camera angles

Unlike Caligarism, German expressionist films such as FW Murnau's *Nosferatu* (1922), used real locations, creating unease with exaggerated shadows, high-contrast lighting and off-kilter camera angles in an attempt to externalise the psychological state. The plots and stories of the films often dealt with madness, insanity and betrayal.

German film historian Lotte Eisner, in her influential book on expressionist cinema, *The Haunted Screen* (1974), argued that the German cinema was a development of 19th-century German romanticism, and that 'modern technique merely lends visible form to Romantic fancies'. Other writers saw dark and moody films like Fritz Lang's *Dr Mabuse, The Gambler* (1922) and *M* (1931), with their sadistic protagonists and nightmarish urban landscapes, as foreshadowing the Third Reich. In the former, the evil, power-mad villain expresses sentiments too close for Nazi comfort, while the child molester and murderer (Peter Lorre) in the latter, seen mostly in silhouette, was said to express the 'German Volksgeist'.

Murnau uses chiaroscuro lighting in *Nosferatu*, establishing stark contrasts between light and dark, the natural and the supernatural, the rational and the irrational. Added to this is the spectral gaunt figure of Max Schreck, as the screen's first Dracula (renamed Count Orlok for copyright reasons), one of the eeriest characters in cinema history.

In contrast was the exquisite bob-haired Louise Brooks exerting her kittenish femme fatale fascination in GW Pabst's *Pandora's Box* and *Diary of a Lost Girl* (both 1929). These indictments of the decadence of the Weimar Republic were more realistic, though Pabst employed expressionistic techniques. However, Pabst's most expressionistic film was *Secrets of a Soul* (1926), with its stunning depiction of dreams told to a psychoanalyst. It contains multilayer superimpositions and menacing images of razors and knives, plainly an influence on Alfred Hitchcock. This can be seen in Hitchcock films from *The Lodger* (1927) to *Psycho* (1960). However, the greatest influence of German expressionism can be seen on Hollywood horror films, especially Tod Browning's *Dracula* (1931), helped enormously by the camerawork of Karl Freund who had shot films for Murnau

and Lang in Germany, and on film noir works, some directed by émigré filmmakers such as Lang, Robert Siodmak and Jacques Tourneur.

German expressionist stylistic elements continued to reappear in the films of Orson Welles, and in Ingmar Bergman's *Sawdust and Tinsel* (1953). The spectacular cityscapes in Ridley Scott's *Blade Runner* (1982) are reminiscent of Lang's *Metropolis* (1927), as are the designs of Gotham City in Tim Burton's *Batman Returns* (1992), in which the villain (Christopher Walken) is named Max Shrek (sic).

KEY WORKS

← **Nosferatu,** 1922, FW MURNAU
Having risen from his coffin, Count Orlok (Max Shreck) arrives in Bremen from Transylvania in a ship stricken by the plague. The chiaroscuro lighting by the cinematographer Fritz Arno Wagner and the make-up by Albin Grau – bat-like ears, fangs and long claws – add to the eeriness of the film.

↙ **M,** 1931, FRITZ LANG
As a psychopathic child-murderer on the loose in Berlin, Peter Lorre gives the defining performance of his career. His bulbous eyes reflecting terror and self-loathing in equal measure are at the centre of Fritz Lang's low-keyed expressionism in which fear permeates every brick of the dark alleys and crumbling buildings.

OTHER WORKS
Dr Mabuse, The Gambler, 1922, LANG; **Variety,** 1925, DUPONT; **Metropolis,** 1927, LANG; **Secrets of a Soul,** 1926, PABST; **The Lodger,** 1927, HITCHCOCK; **Diary of a Lost Girl,** 1929, PABST; **Pandora's Box,** 1929, PABST; **The Blue Angel,** 1930, STERNBERG; **Dracula,** 1931, BROWNING; **Frankenstein,** 1931, WHALE; **Sawdust and Tinsel,** 1953, BERGMAN; **Psycho,** 1960, HITCHCOCK; **Blade Runner,** 1982, RIDLEY SCOTT; **Batman Returns,** 1992, BURTON

Illusionism; Caligarism; Horrorism; Surrealism; Film Noirism

Constructivism; Escapism; Costume Romanticism; Musicalism; Classicism

From the start of the Russian Revolution in 1917, there was an unprecedented explosion of creativity in all the arts. The constructivists sought to reaffirm Soviet society through art. The new medium of cinema seemed ideal for such a purpose by creating a revolutionary effect mainly through montage.

DZIGA VERTOV 1896–1954; **SERGEI EISENSTEIN** 1898–1948; **LEV KULESHOV** 1899-1970; **BORIS BARNET** 1902-1965; **LEONID TRAUBERG** 1902–90; **GRIGORI KOZINTSEV** 1905–73

anti-bourgeois; design; formalism; montage; practicality; propaganda

The constructivists were at the forefront of the movement to bring art into union with life, rejecting the bourgeois doctrine of 'art for art's sake', and believing in the integration of art with the reconstruction of society. They believed in Lenin's phrase that 'the function of cinema is to maintain revolutionary fervour'. Therefore many artists moved from painting, sculpture and theatre into cinema. For example, the radical poet Vladimir Mayakovsky co-wrote, co-directed and starred in Yevgeni Slavinsky's *The Young Lady and the Hooligan* (1918). Many filmmakers expressed their attraction to jazz-age America (though not its politics), and admiration for comedians like Charlie Chaplin or Buster Keaton, as well as Fordist mass production, all of which was demonstrated by Lev Kuleshov's *The Extraordinary Adventures of Mr West in the Land of the Bolsheviks* (1924).

Sergei Eisenstein, an engineer by education, once stated that: 'I approach the making of a motion picture in much the

same way as I would approach the installation of a water system.' Leonid Trauberg and Grigori Kozintsev, who founded the Factory of the Eccentric Actor (FECS) group, shifted their activities from stage to the cinema in 1924, the same year Eisenstein made his first feature, *The Strike*, in which many of the stylistic devices of constructivism were in evidence – caricatures, visual metaphors and dynamic cutting which Eisenstein referred to as the 'montage of attractions'. This reached its peak in Eisenstein's *The Battleship Potemkin* (1925), and especially in the celebrated 'Odessa Steps' sequence.

Dziga Vertov (born Denis Kaufman) edited *Kino-Pravda* (Cinema Truth) and *Kino-Glaz* (Cinema Eye), a series of documentary films created from newsreels, between 1922 and 1925 to which he added slow, speeded-up and reverse motion, split screens, animation, text and still photographs. These techniques and more were used in his masterpiece *Man With a Movie Camera* (1929), a spectacular constructivist celluloid poem depicting everyday Soviet city life, and celebrating man and machine.

Yakov Protazanov's science-fiction film *Aelita* (1924), a didactic comedy with futuristic sets designed by Sergei Kozlovsky, told of a small group of Russians who land on Mars and organise a revolution on the Soviet model against the autocratic ruler. It optimistically views the future from the USSR's new economic policy, while Trauberg and Kozintsev in *The New Babylon* (1929) see it through the prism of the past. This dazzlingly inventive satire, set in Paris during the Commune of 1871, used montage and lighting to contrast the rich and the poor. Alas, the arrival of sound coincided with the development of socialist realism and a reaction against formalism in the arts.

KEY WORKS

↑ **The Battleship Potemkin,** 1925, SERGEI EISENSTEIN
A shot from the 'Odessa Steps' sequence shows soldiers advancing on the fleeing citizens down a seemingly endless flight of steps. A mother carrying her dead child towards the soldiers in a plea for mercy creates a sudden poignant counterpoint to the main flow of the crowds. For Eisenstein, force (thesis) colliding with counterforce (antithesis) produces unity (synthesis).

← **Man with a Movie Camera,** 1929, DZIGA VERTOV
Vertov's brother, Mikhail Kaufman, is superimposed on a crane above an unnamed city. He is seen in multiple locations, often in impossible situations, as he captures a kaleidoscope of the inhabitants and the machines that keep the city moving. Using all the techniques of cinema at his disposal, Vertov celebrates the Soviet Union's integration of man and machine.

OTHER WORKS
The Young Lady and the Hooligan, 1918, SLAVINSKY; Kino-Pravda (Cinema Truth) and Kino-Glaz (Cinema Eye), 1922–5, VERTOV; The Strike, 1924, EISENSTEIN; Aelita, 1924, PROTAZANOV; The Extraordinary Adventures of Mr West in the Land of the Bolsheviks, 1924, KULESHOV; The House on Trubnaya Square, 1928, BARNET; The New Babylon, 1929, TRAUBERG/KOZINTZEV

 Documentarism; Avant-Gardism; Propagandism; Utopianism; New Wavism

 Classicism; Socialist Realism; Italian Neo-Realism; Film Noirism; Revisionism

🕐 There has always been a flood of filmmakers who have attempted, in various ways, to capture 'truth' on celluloid, whether they call it documentary, non-fiction, factual, *Kino-Pravda*, *Cinéma Verité* or Direct Cinema.

◑ **ROBERT FLAHERTY** 1884–1951; **RICHARD LEACOCK** 1921–; **CHRIS MARKER** 1921–; **ALAIN RESNAIS** 1922–; **CLAUDE LANZMANN** 1925–; **ALBERT MAYSLES** 1926–; **MARCEL OPHÜLS** 1927–; **FRED WISEMAN** 1930–; **DAVID MAYSLES** 1932–87; **ERROL MORRIS** 1948–; **MICHAEL MOORE** 1954–

◑ interviews; long shots; natural locations and lighting; newsreel footage; static camera; voice-over

⚫ Documentarism takes several forms: propagandistic, educational, lyrical, experimental, subjective and objective. Many documentaries seek to persuade an audience to a particular point of view by a careful selection of facts, generally to make people aware of certain deleterious social conditions. When reality is distorted to fit an argument, the film could be considered as propaganda. On the whole, however, documentarists claim that they do not create a world so much as report on the existing one.

The term was first applied by John Grierson to Robert Flaherty's *Moana* (1926). Grierson, the leading force behind the British documentary movement in the 1930s, defined documentary as 'the creative treatment of actuality'. Documentaries only began to be taken seriously immediately after the Russian Revolution (1917) when propaganda pictures were sent across the vast country to convert the people to Bolshevism. In contrast were Flaherty's ethnological documentaries such as *Nanook of the North* (1922), although he did get the Inuit family to re-enact some scenes for the camera. Flaherty's influence on the documentary is felt in Merian C Cooper and Ernest B Schoedsack's adventure-travel films *Grass* (1925) and *Chang* (1927).

The outbreak of the Second World War took documentary filmmakers into the field of propaganda. The end of the war saw a drop in the output of documentary films in the West because they had become too closely associated with propaganda, and because television took over their role. But in England in the 1950s, the so-called Free Cinema – a series of objective shorts describing mostly working-class people and places – launched the careers of Lindsay Anderson, Karel Reisz and Tony Richardson. In France, Alain Resnais made several remarkable shorts, among them *Night and Fog* (1955), his devastating film about Nazi concentration camps, in which black-and-white archive material is intercut with contemporary footage in colour.

Resnais' film belongs to the category of documentaries dealing with historical fact used for investigative exposés. These include films such as Marcel Ophüls' *The Sorrow and The Pity* (1969), a portrait of France under German occupation, and Claude Lanzmann's *Shoah* (1985) on the Holocaust. *The Thin Blue Line* (1988), Errol Morris' investigation into a 1976 murder, helped free an innocent man from death row.

The basis of *Cinéma Verité* in France, led by Jean Rouch and Chris Marker, and Direct Cinema in America, instigated by the Maysles brothers, Albert and David, Richard Leacock and Fred Wiseman, was that the camera should record people's behaviour as unobtrusively as possible. This was made possible by the invention of a lightweight, hand-held 16-millimetre camera, synced to a quiet recorder. The style was imitated for semi-documentaries (with actors) and comic mockumentaries. Documentaries of all types underwent a renaissance at the beginning of the 21st century with Michael Moore's personal exposé films entering the mainstream.

KEY WORKS

↗ **Fahrenheit 9/11**, 2004, MICHAEL MOORE
Moore put himself at the centre of his angry serio-comic investigations into social ills. Here he associates with an Iraqi war veteran in his scathing take on the Bush administration and its much touted 'War on Terror'. The film was the first documentary to win a Golden Palm at Cannes.

← **Nanook of the North**, 1922, ROBERT FLAHERTY
Nanook, an Inuit living with his family in harsh conditions in Canada's Hudson Bay, re-enacts the past practice of the hunting of a walrus for Flaherty's camera. In the first full-length anthropological film, which had its basis in reality, an unprecedented rapport was created between the subjects and the man behind the camera.

OTHER WORKS

Grass, 1925, COOPER/SCHOEDSACK; **Moana**, 1926, FLAHERTY; **Chang**, 1927, COOPER/SCHOEDSACK; **Night and Fog**, 1955, RESNAIS; **The Sorrow and the Pity**, 1969, OPHÜLS; **Shoah**, 1985, LANZMANN; **The Emperor's Naked Army Marches On**, 1987, HARA ; **The Thin Blue Line**, 1988, MORRIS; **Étre et avoir**, 2002, PHILIBERT; **Modern Life**, 2008, DEPARDON

 Anti-Militarism; Propagandism; Naturalism; Realism; Italian Neo-Realism

 Illusionism; Expressionism; Hollywood Studioism; Escapism; Costume Romanticism

◐ In cinema, avant-garde specifically refers to a group of influential and radical filmmakers who were active in Europe from the end of the First World War.

● **WALTER RUTTMANN** 1887–1941; **HANS RICHTER** 1888–1976; **LOUIS DELLUC** 1890–1924; **MARCEL L'HERBIER** 1890–1979; **JEAN EPSTEIN** 1897–1953

◑ abstraction; complex allusions; formalistic; fragmentary images; non-linear narratives

● In Europe in the 1920s, film began to attract artists from the visual arts. Avant-garde artists like Man Ray, Hans Richter, Fernand Léger, Oskar Fischinger and Walter Ruttmann made films influenced by German expressionism and Russian constructivism, though they abandoned notions of narrative, attempting to put 'paintings in motion'.

Richter's *Rhythmus 21* (1921–4), Ruttmann's *Opus I–IV* (1921–5) and Léger's *Ballet mécanique* (1924) aspired towards 'visual music', as did Fischinger's *Circles* (1932) and *Motion Painting* (1947), which synchronised abstract patterns to the music of Wagner and Bach. Man Ray directed a number of influential avant-garde short films, known as *Cinéma Pur* (Pure Cinema), such as *Les mystères du château de Dé* (1929).

Richter teamed up with Ray, Léger, Marcel Duchamp, Max Ernst and the composer John Cage to make the feature-length *Dreams That Money Can Buy* (1947), an anthology piece for which each of its co-creators tackled their own individual segment within the framing device of a would-be poet who discovers the power to summon up dreams for others.

Ruttmann broke from his earlier 'absolute' films with *Berlin: Symphony of a*

Great City (1927), an impressionistic view of life in the German capital on a spring day from dawn to midnight. Edmund Meisel, who composed the jazzy score (since lost), worked with the director on the editing to give it a rhythmic effect. The film, influenced by the developments of Soviet montage, led to further avant-garde documentaries in a similar vein, including Dziga Vertov's constructivist *Man With a Movie Camera* (1929).

In contrast, the early films of Marcel L'Herbier have plots, though they are full of avant-garde innovations. In *El Dorado* (1921), blurred image *(flou)* and multiple superimpositions are used, and each set for *L'inhumaine* (1924) was created by a different designer, including Léger, and featured dancers from the Ballet Suedois and music by Darius Milhaud. *L'argent* (1928), based on Émile Zola's (1891) novel of the same name, was L'Herbier's most ambitious film, a three-hour condemnation of big business with an international cast moving through huge modernist sets.

Jean Epstein recreated the eerie poetry of the Edgar Allan Poe story in *The Fall of the House of Usher* (1928), in which slow motion was probably used for the first time in a fiction film.

The spirit of the avant-garde lived on in France in the films of Chris Marker, the husband-and-wife team of Jean-Marie Straub and Danielle Huillet, and in those of Peter Greenaway in England and in the American Underground of the 1960s, which included the works of Andy Warhol, who created his own 'factory' and 'superstars', as well as films such as *Sleep* (1963) – one take of a man sleeping for six hours.

KEY WORKS

← **L'inhumaine,** 1924, MARCEL L'HERBIER
This film would create a synthesis of avant-garde art of the mid-1920s, with sets and costumes by the leading modernist artists of the day. Here, the engineer (Jaque Catelain), hopelessly in love with a soprano (Georgette Leblanc), 'the inhuman one' of the title, wanders distraught through the impluvium (designed by Fernand Léger) of the house where she presides over a salon of men.

↙ **Berlin: Symphony of a Great City,** 1927, WALTER RUTTMANN
A collage effect created for this visual poem on the everyday life of the bustling city of Berlin just prior to the coming of power by the Nazis.

OTHER WORKS
El Dorado, 1921, L'HERBIER; Rhythmus 21, 1921–4, RICHTER; Opus I–IV, 1921–5, RUTTMANN; The Woman From Nowhere (La femme de nulle part), 1922, DELLUC; Ballet mécanique, 1924, LÉGER; L'argent, 1928, L'HERBIER; The Fall of the House of Usher, 1928, EPSTEIN; Les mystères du château de Dé, 1929, MAN RAY; Circles, 1932, FISCHINGER; Dreams That Money Can Buy, 1947, RICHTER; Motion Painting, 1947, FISCHINGER; Sleep, 1963, WARHOL; From the Clouds to the Resistance, 1979, STRAUB/HUILLET; The Falls, 1981, GREENAWAY; Sunless, 1983, MARKER

 Expressionism; Constructivism; Surrealism; Experimentalism; New Wavism

 Hollywood Studioism; Socialist Realism; Realism; Classicism; Emotionalism

2

THE FIRST
SOUND DECADE
1928–38

From the early 1920s to the late 1950s, the Hollywood studio system dominated cinema. By concentrating production into vast factory-like studios – dubbed 'dream factories' – and by handling all aspects of the business, from production to publicity to distribution to exhibition, these studios were able to control the world market.

CARL LAEMMLE 1867–1939; ADOLPH ZUKOR 1873–1976; LOUIS B MAYER 1884–1957; HARRY COHN 1891–1958; IRVING THALBERG 1899–1936; JACK WARNER 1892–1978;

contract staff; cost effective; individual studio style; star system

Around 1910, a number of film companies, run mainly by a handful of streetwise Jewish immigrants, set up business in the small suburb of Hollywood to the west of Los Angeles. Within a decade the system they created came to dominate the cinema, not only in the US but throughout the world. The factory-like studios developed cost-effective methods of production and ensured the flow of films from producer to consumer by acquiring ownership of theatres at home and abroad, thus creating a monopoly on screen entertainment.

Each of the major studios, with their distinctive logos, developed a characteristic style with its own roster of directors, stars,

KEY WORKS

← **Grand Hotel,** EDMUND GOULDING/MGM, 1932
MGM was able to draw on its vast resources for this glossy multi-star vehicle set in a luxury hotel in Berlin, with art design and costumes by Cedric Gibbons and Adrian respectively. Greta Garbo as a melancholy Russian ballerina, despite wanting to be alone, falls for penniless Baron John Barrymore, here showing his famous profile.

designers and technicians who dictated the look and sound of the films. MGM, with its huge financial resources, was the most glamorous. Under the leadership of Louis B Mayer and Irving Thalberg, the studio specialised in family entertainment such as *Singin' in The Rain* (1952), only rarely venturing into controversial themes. Their boast that MGM had 'more stars in the heavens' was demonstrated by films such as *Grand Hotel* (1932).

With its decorative opulence, Paramount, headed by Adolph Zukor, was the most European of the studios, employing several leading foreign-born directors including Josef von Sternberg and Ernst Lubitsch. Among the American directors at Paramount was one of its founder members, Cecil B DeMille, who became known for his historical and biblical epics. and Billy Wilder, who included DeMille and the studio in *Sunset Boulevard* (1950)

In sharp contrast was Warner Bros, under boss Jack Warner, which was more in tune with the working class. Notorious for frugality, no studio better evoked the Depression, both in the content and look of its films. The studio's memorable cycle of gangster movies and social dramas reflected the mood of the period. Even Warner Bros musicals were hard-edged. Perhaps the most memorable of Warner studio productions was *Casablanca* (1943), where all the elements came together.

Universal Pictures, run by Carl Laemmle, became associated in the public's mind with horror movies with its vivid monsters played by Bela Lugosi and Boris Karloff.

Among the smaller studios was Columbia, which grew into a major contender thanks to the dynamic leadership of the tyrannical Harry Cohn and the creative talent of Frank Capra. The policy of RKO Radio Pictures was to produce films

capitalising on its contract stars. The most popular were Fred Astaire and Ginger Rogers, whose seductive harmony of movement was given expression in nine musicals between 1933 and 1939.

A latecomer to the majors, Twentieth Century Fox was formed in 1935. The man most responsible for its particular formula, which emphasised technical polish and visual gloss, was Darryl F Zanuck. The studio made most of its money from light-hearted musicals as well as folksy recreations of America's recent past.

Three of the most celebrated Hollywood stars, Douglas Fairbanks, Mary Pickford and Charlie Chaplin, and the great director DW Griffith, unhappy with their lack of independence in working under contract to others, formed United Artists (UA). Unlike other big companies, UA had no specific studio location, contract players or technical staff, but acted as patron and distribution company to many independent producers.

→ **Sunset Boulevard** 1950, BILLY WILDER
'I am big. It's the pictures that got small,' says Gloria Swanson as forgotten silent star Norma Desmond. Wilder's film ambiguously juxtaposed Hollywood's baroque past with the brash new generation.

OTHER WORKS
Dracula, 1931, BROWNING/UNIVERSAL; **I Am A Fugitive From A Chain Gang,** 1932, LEROY/WARNER BROS; **Design for Living,** 1933, LUBITSCH/PARAMOUNT; **42nd Street,** 1933, BACON/WARNER BROS; **It Happened One Night,** 1934, CAPRA/COLUMBIA; **Top Hat,** 1935, SANDRICH/RKO RADIO PICTURES; **Casablanca,** 1943, CURTIZ/WARNER BROS; **Singin' In The Rain,** 1952, KELLY/DONEN/MGM; **How To Marry A Millionaire,** 1953, NEGULESCO/TWENTIETH CENTURY FOX

 Gangsterism; Escapism; Westernism; Musicalism; Classicism

 Avant-Gardism; New Wavism; Auteurism; Minimalism; Dogmetism; American Indieism

Horrorism

Films that seek to create terror in the audience have had a long history in the cinema. Ranging from the intimation of horrors to the depiction of graphic violence, they offer a form of catharsis by tapping into our deepest fears and anxieties.

PAUL WEGENER 1874–1948; TOD BROWNING 1880–1962; PAUL LENI 1885–1929; JAMES WHALE 1889–1957; ALFRED HITCHCOCK 1899–1980; VAL LEWTON 1904–51; JACQUES TOURNEUR 1904–77; MARIO BAVA 1914–80; ROGER CORMAN 1926–; DARIO ARGENTO 1940–; GEORGE A ROMERO 1940–; KIYOSHI KUROSAWA 1955–; TAKASHI MIIKE 1960–; HIDEO NAKATA 1961–

eerie music; grotesque make-up; off-screen diegetic sound; shadows; special effects

Horror films deal with our fears of violence and death, as well as the dread of the unknown, such as the mysteries of the spiritual world. Audiences seem to get pleasure from following events that normally exist in the unconscious or in nightmares. While it is essential to identify with the characters in jeopardy on screen (usually attractive women), there is the satisfaction of feeling secure in one's seat at the same time. The genre has two main strands: those that feature monsters (vampires, werewolves, zombies) and those that involve ghosts, usually in a haunted house.

The films of terror were informed by a crystallisation of influences, the major ones being the British Gothic novels of the 18th and 19th centuries such as Mary Shelly's *Frankenstein*, Bram Stoker's *Dracula* and Robert Louis Stevenson's *Dr Jeykll and Mr Hyde* – all favourites of the cinema – and, by the late 18th and early 19th century, German romanticism in all the arts. The latter shaped German expressionist films like *The Cabinet of Dr Caligari* (1919) and *Nosferatu* (1921),

which, in turn, influenced the Hollywood horror films that reached their acme in the 1930s. For example, Boris Karloff's lumbering gait as Frankenstein's monster was taken from the performance by Paul Wegener in *The Golem* (1920), which he co-directed.

Although Hollywood benefited from the presence of European émigrés such as Paul Leni (*The Cat and the Canary*, 1927) and Karl Freund (*The Mummy*, 1932), the two most notable horror films made in the US at the beginning of the sound era were directed by an American, Tod Browning (*Dracula*, 1931) and an Englishman, James Whale (*Frankenstein*, 1931). Helped by actors Béla Lugosi and Boris Karloff, they set the style for the cycle of horror films, mainly for Universal Studios. Browning had previously made eight frightening silent movies with Lon Chaney, who specialised in portraying grotesques.

During the 1940s, the real horrors of the Second World War made monster movies seem innocuous by comparison. However, the chillers produced by Val Lewton at RKO relied on what is suggested being more frightening than what is revealed. The underlying fear of the supernatural invested each scene in Jacques Tourneur's *Cat People* (1942) and *I Walked with a Zombie* (1943). Britain's Hammer Studios brought all the notorious monsters back to life in gory Technicolor in the 1950s and 1960s, while Roger Corman produced a series of garish adaptations of Edgar Allan Poe's short stories, such as *The Masque of the Red Death* (1964). In the 1960s and 1970s, Italy produced a stream of startling baroque movies directed by Mario Bava and Dario Argento, while the US delved deeper and deeper into gore.

Japan is the one country that has produced more horror films than any other.

Unlike their Western counterparts, the origin of the Japanese horror films (often referred to as 'J-horror') can be traced to ghost story classics of the past centuries. Among the most prominent directors of J-horror are Kiyoshi Kurosawa and Takashi Miike. At the beginning of the 21st century, based on the success of Hideo Nakata's *The Ring* (1998), several Japanese horror films were remade in America.

KEY WORKS

Frankenstein, JAMES WHALE, 1931 [see p.34]
The British James Whale chose his compatriot Boris Karloff (born William Henry Pratt) for the role of the monster. Although one of the most famous of horror movies, it is full of self-mocking black humour, and at its centre is the touching poetic performance from Karloff with iconic make-up devised by Jack Pierce with the famous bolts on the neck which are actually electrodes.

↑ **The Masque of the Red Death,** ROGER CORMAN, 1964
Vincent Price as the 12th-century Prince Prospero, a depraved Satanist who vainly tries to prevent the figure of the Red Death from entering his castle. Director

Roger Corman took the blackly humorous tone of his Edgar Allan Poe adaptations from Price's sibillant ghoulish hamming. The team of designer Daniel Haller and cameraman Floyd Crosby was able to create sumptuous settings on a small budget.

OTHER WORKS

The Golem, 1920, BOESE/WEGENER; **The Phantom of the Opera,** 1925, JULIAN; **The Cat and the Canary,** 1927, LENI; **Dracula,** 1931, BROWNING; **Frankenstein,** 1931, WHALE; **The Mummy,** 1932, FREUND; **Vampyr,** 1932, DREYER; **The Bride of Frankenstein,** 1935, WHALE; **Cat People,** 1942, TOURNEUR; **I Walked with a Zombie,** 1943, TOURNEUR; **Les diaboliques,** 1955, CLOUZOT; **Black Sunday,** 1960, BAVA; **Psycho,** 1960, HITCHCOCK; **The Haunting,** 1963, WISE; **Kwaidan,** 1964, KOBAYASHI; **Night of the Living Dead,** 1968, ROMERO; **Rosemary's Baby,** 1968, POLANSKI; **The Exorcist,** 1973, FRIEDKIN; **The Ring,** 1998, NAKATA

 Illusionism; Caligarism; Expressionism; Surrealism; FX-ism

 Screwballism; Utopianism; Realism; Musicalism; Feminism

The French poet André Breton argued in his surrealist manifesto (1924) for art 'in the absence of any control exercised by reason, exempt from any aesthetic or moral concern'. Naturally, cinema, seemed an ideal medium to realise Breton's theories.

JEAN COCTEAU 1889–1963; LUIS BUÑUEL 1900–83; WOJCIECH HAS 1925–2000; ROY ANDERSSON 1943–; DAVID LYNCH 1946–; CHARLIE KAUFMAN 1958–

dreams; eroticism; irrationality; mirror images; nonlinear

Jean Cocteau described cinema as 'not a dream that is told but one we all dream together', which fitted in with the surrealists' concept of art as 'psychic automatism', a free play of the mind and the subconscious. The films expressed the irrational, neurotic and the chaotic.

Surrealist painters such as Salvador Dalí, Fernard Léger, Man Ray and Marcel Duchamp all dabbled in films, the latter two appearing in the first surrealist film, René Clair's *Entr'acte* (1924), which uses speeded-up motion and balletic slow motion as it follows a number of crazy characters who end up at a funeral chasing a runaway hearse. Man Ray's *L'étoile de mer* (*Star Fish*, 1928) masterfully employs stark surrealist imagery and unsettling naturalistic photography as it alternates between dreams and reality with obvious references to subconscious sexual desire.

Dalí and Luis Buñuel co-conceived *Un chien andalou* (1928), which has one of the most startling of openings of any film – an eye being slashed by a razor. Dalí again contributed much to *L'âge d'or* (*The Golden Age*, 1930), which has two lovers constantly having their sexual desires thwarted by

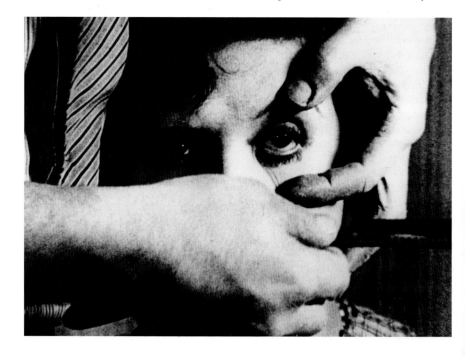

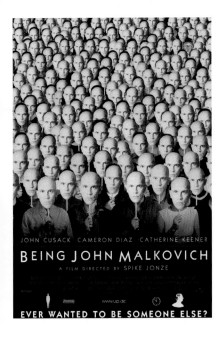

JOHN CUSACK · CAMERON DIAZ · CATHERINE KEENER

BEING JOHN MALKOVICH

A FILM DIRECTED BY SPIKE JONZE

www.up.de

EVER WANTED TO BE SOMEONE ELSE?

such as Walerian Borowczyk and Wojciech Has in Poland, and Jan Švankmajer in Czechoslovakia. Surreal humour pervaded the Swede Roy Andersson's *Songs from the Second Floor* (2000) and *You, the Living* (2007). In the US, David Lynch often refers to André Breton as a mentor and quotes his ideas about *les merveilleux banal* (the wonder of the mundane), and screenwriter Charlie Kaufman has taken American films into new surrealist zones, for example with *Being John Malkovich* (1999).

KEY WORKS

← **Being John Malkovich,** 1999, SPIKE JONZE
John Malkovich is multiplied a hundred-fold in his own imagination after a struggling puppeteer (John Cusack) discovers a secret portal that allows him to enter the mind of the actor for 15 minutes. The surreal jokes include an office on the seventh-and-a-half floor with 5-foot-3-inch ceilings, and Malkovich playing himself as vain and lustful.

← **Un chien andalou,** 1928, LUIS BUÑUEL
The shocking opening sequence in which a girl's eye seems to be slit by a razor, one of many memorable surrealistic images in a film of unconnected incidents designed to follow the logic of a dream.

bourgeois society. Buñuel was the surrealist par excellence, never wavering in his anti-bourgeois and anti-clerical ideas and mordantly comic vision.

Although Cocteau dissociated himself from the surrealists, his films, from *The Blood of the Poet* (1930) to *The Testament of Orpheus* (1960), use much of the dream imagery of the movement. It was Cocteau who inspired the films of Underground filmmaker Kenneth Anger, especially the homo-erotic *Fireworks* (1947). Elements of surrealism also influenced more mainstream movies such as *Duck Soup* (1933) in which the Marx Brothers' uninhibited madcap behaviour conveyed a sense of spontaneity. In fact, in 1937, Dalí wrote a screenplay (unfilmed) for the comedians entitled *Giraffes on Horseback Salads*.

Surrealism, with its cryptic symbols, attracted many Eastern European film directors working under repressive regimes,

OTHER WORKS
Entr'acte, 1924, CLAIR; La coquille et le clergyman (The Seashell and the Clergyman), 1928, DULAC; L'étoile de mer (Star Fish), 1928, MAN RAY; L'âge d'or (The Golden Age), 1930, BUÑUEL; The Blood of the Poet, 1930, COCTEAU; Duck Soup, 1933, MCCAREY; Fireworks, 1947, ANGER; Orphée, 1950, COCTEAU; The Testament of Orpheus, 1960, COCTEAU; Last Year at Marienbad, 1961, RESNAIS; The Discreet Charm of the Bourgeoisie, 1972, BUÑUEL; Eraserhead, 1977, LYNCH; Blue Velvet, 1986, LYNCH; Songs from the Second Floor, 2000, ANDERSSON; You, the Living, 2007, ANDERSSON

 Illusionism; Expressionism; Avant-Gardism; Horrorism; Experimentalism

 Costume Romanticism; Socialist Realism; Naturalism; Italian Neo-Realism; Classicism

Gangsterism

🕐 amorality; cryptic plots; double-crossings; slangy dialogue; violence

● The gangster movie as a distinct genre came into its own with the coming of sound and the Warner Bros cycle launched with Mervyn LeRoy's *Little Caesar* (1930), William Wellman's *The Public Enemy* (1931) and Howard Hawks' *Scarface* (1932). These three films set the pattern for future crime movies. Though the moral perspective altered over the years, the iconographic elements – the urban setting, violence, the rise and fall of a brutal, ambitious hoodlum, the moll, the crusading newspaper man, the shyster lawyer, the nightclub and the car chase – remained more or less intact.

During the Depression, with stars like Edward G Robinson, James Cagney, George Raft and Humphrey Bogart, audiences saw gangsters as folk heroes, striving against 'respectable' society. 'The gangster is the "no" to the great American "yes" which is stamped so large over our official culture', wrote Robert Warshaw in *The Gangster as Tragic Hero* (1948). This produced an outcry in some influential quarters against the somewhat sympathetic

🕐 The favourite period of Hollywood gangsterism was Prohibition America of the 1920s when racketeers flourished. The ground rules of the genre were laid down with the coming of sound, and evolved throughout a variety of eras and nations, allowing filmmakers to use its conventions to comment upon social, ethnographic and political issues.

◖ EDWARD G ROBINSON 1893–1973; GEORGE RAFT 1895–1980; HUMPHREY BOGART 1899–1957; JAMES CAGNEY 1899–1986; JEAN-PIERRE MELVILLE 1917–73; JOHN WOO 1946–; TAKESHI KITANO 1947–; JOHNNIE TO 1955–; QUENTIN TARANTINO 1963–)

and glamorous approach to such real-life figures as Al Capone, John Dillinger and 'Legs' Diamond. In 1934, the newly established Production Code stated that 'crime will be shown to be wrong and that the criminal life will be loathed and that the law will at all times prevail'. This led to a rash of police-enforcement films with more condemnatory portraits. In Michael Curtiz's *Angels with Dirty Faces* (1938), Cagney pretends to turn yellow when facing the electric chair to prevent the Dead End Kids, who idolise him, from following in his footsteps.

The gangster film almost disappeared during the Second World War; Hitler had exceeded anything Hollywood had dreamt up for its hoodlums. When it re-emerged, there was more emphasis on the psychological, as in Raoul Walsh's *White Heat* (1949), which starred Cagney as a mother-fixated killer.

The genre was taken up by low-budget director Roger Corman, who focused on the more sensational aspects of the plots, and in France and Japan in the 1960s. Both Jean-Luc Godard and François Truffaut have paid homage to the American gangster movie, while Jean-Pierre Melville's characters double-cross and kill as they move ceremoniously through sleazy Parisian bars, hotels and clubs, but nevertheless have a code of honour. As one character says of the gangster in *Second Breath* (1966): 'He is a danger to society, but he has preserved a sort of purity.'

This chimed well with Akira Kurosawa's crime movies such as *The Bad Sleep Well* (1960) and *High and Low* (1963), and with the various *yakuza* (Japanese organised crime) films by the likes of Seijun Suzuki, Kinji Fukasaku, Takashi Miike and Takeshi Kitano, and the triad films of Hong Kong by Johnnie To and John Woo.

Hollywood gangsterism became more ambiguous after Arthur Penn's *Bonnie and Clyde* (1967), with its amoral attitude to the outlaw seen from a modern psychological and social viewpoint. It opened the way for Francis Ford Coppola's *The Godfather* trilogy (1972, 1974 and 1990) and Martin Scorsese's hoods. It was Quentin Tarantino who gave gangsterism a postmodern twist in *Reservoir Dogs* (1992) and *Pulp Fiction* (1994), divorcing it from the world outside the cinema.

KEY WORKS

← **Scarface,** 1932, HOWARD HAWKS
Paul Muni (centre), flanked by his simple cohort Vince Barnett and his moll Karen Morley, shows his ruthlessness. Based on the life of racketeer Al Capone, the film was rejected by critics and the public on its release but is now considered a classic of the genre. Muni is at once brutish, childish, arrogant, sinister and often touching in the title role.

→ **The Godfather: Part II,** 1974, FRANCIS FORD COPPOLA
Al Pacino as Michael Corleone moves gradually from being the wide-eyed youngest brother of the clan to controlled coldness and deadpan calculation which he puts to bloody use in the service of the family. With extraordinary chiaroscuro photography of the interiors, Coppola builds up a rich pattern of relationships detailing the rituals of an enclosed group.

OTHER WORKS

Little Caesar, 1930, LEROY; **The Public Enemy,** 1931, WELLMAN; **Angels with Dirty Faces,** 1938, CURTIZ; **White Heat,** 1949, WALSH; **The Bad Sleep Well,** 1960, KUROSAWA; **High and Low,** 1963, KUROSAWA; **Second Breath,** 1966, MELVILLE; **Bonnie and Clyde,** 1967, PENN; **Le Samurai,** 1967, MELVILLE; **Reservoir Dogs,** 1992, TARANTINO; **Pulp Fiction,** 1994, TARANTINO

 Naturalism; Realism; Film Noirism; Revisionism; Postmodernism

 Illusionism; Screwballism; Costume Romanticism; Utopianism; Emotionalism

Screwballism

Screwball comedy was a unique creation of Hollywood in the 1930s and early 1940s, its main elements being irreverent humour, fast-paced action and dialogue, eccentric characters, the battle of the sexes and a clash between the idle rich and the more practical poor.

GREGORY LA CAVA 1892–1952; HOWARD HAWKS 1896–1977; MITCHELL LEISEN 1897–1972; FRANK CAPRA 1897–1991; PRESTON STURGES 1898–1959; LEO MCCAREY 1898–1969; GEORGE CUKOR 1899–1983; CLAUDETTE COLBERT 1903–96; CARY GRANT 1904–86; CAROLE LOMBARD 1908–42

battle of the sexes; eccentric characters; fast-paced ; improbable plots; irreverent humour; witty dialogue

As screwball comedy emerged from the Great Depression, it is understandable that one of its main themes was the idle rich learning how the other half lives. Gently satiric, the films often ended with the bonding of the wealthy heroine with the proletarian hero after initial hostility. A typical example is Gregory La Cava's *My Man Godfrey* (1936), a variation on James Barrie's *The Admirable Crichton* (1902). It tells of how a man (William Powell) from a Hooverville (shanty town) becomes butler to a wealthy family, straightens out their lives and marries the scatterbrained daughter (played by Carole Lombard, a screwball favourite). Frank Capra's *It Happened One Night* (1934) was about a spoiled runaway heiress (played by Claudette Colbert) having to rough it with a hard-boiled reporter (Clark Gable) on her tail.

George Cukor's *Holiday* (1938) features an impecunious Cary Grant, engaged to the snobby daughter of a millionaire banker who discovers the girl he really loves is her unconventional sister (Katharine Hepburn). Instead of accepting a lucrative job, he takes off with the sister to Europe, both giving up their gilded existence.

divorce and then remarry one another – for example, Leo McCarey's *The Awful Truth* (1937) and Cukor's *The Philadelphia Story* (1940) – showing a more liberated attitude to divorce.

Screwball comedy continued into the 1940s in a similar vein with Preston Sturges' social comedies. Quintessential was *Palm Beach Story* (1942), in which Claudette Colbert takes off by train for Florida to get a divorce from her insolvent husband (Joel McCrea) and to marry a rich man. However, screwballism ended with the advent of the Second World War when frivolity and class ridicule seemed inappropriate.

KEY WORKS

 My Man Godfrey, 1936, GREGORY LA CAVA
Carole Lombard as the pampered heiress moons over William Powell as Godfrey 'Smith', a businessman ruined by the Depression and forced to become a butler. The film wittily contrasts the poverty of 'forgotten men' with the spoilt lifestyles of the idle rich. Powell and Lombard, who were briefly married from 1931 to 1933, exude real affection for one another.

 It Happened One Night, 1934, FRANK CAPRA
The celebrated 'Walls of Jericho' sequence in which the wacky runaway heiress (Claudette Colbert) and the hard-boiled reporter (Clark Gable) are forced to share a motel room, pretending to be married. They string up blankets between them to act as screens. The film ends with the couple returning on their honeymoon, where a toy trumpet is heard as the blankets fall to the floor, all sexual barriers down.

OTHER WORKS

The Awful Truth, 1937, MCCAREY; Easy Living, 1937, LEISEN; Bringing Up Baby, 1938, HAWKS; Holiday, 1938, CUKOR; His Girl Friday, 1940, HAWKS; My Favorite Wife, 1940, KANIN; The Philadelphia Story, 1940, CUKOR; Palm Beach Story, 1942, PRESTON STURGES; What's Up, Doc?, 1972, BOGDANOVICH

Grant and Hepburn turned out to be the perfect screwball couple, especially in Howard Hawks' *Bringing Up Baby* (1938) where Hepburn is a wacky heiress pursuing Grant as a bespectacled palaeontologist, all played at break-neck speed. The plot, like many other screwball comedies, is consistently as crazy as the protagonists, both operating within a logical non-logic of their own.

Dynamic women feature in a number of screwball comedies in which the heroines behave as independently and aggressively as the male. As Hepburn says of Grant in *Bringing Up Baby*: 'He's the man I'm going to marry, he doesn't know it, but I am.' Hawks' comedies were especially adept at gender role-swapping, such as in *His Girl Friday* (1940) in which Rosalind Russell's ace reporter vainly tries to settle down to middle-class marriage.

The latter falls into the category of comedies of remarriage, in which characters

Slapstickism; Hollywood Studioism; Escapism; Cartoonism; Musicalism

Horrorism; Gangsterism; Poetic Realism; Propagandism; Socialist Realism

Exoticism

Taken from an occidental and Hollywood perspective, oriental countries are considered exotic, especially as seen through the prism of fictional films that play up the exoticism.

ROBERT FLAHERTY 1884–1951; ERIC VON STROHEIM 1885–1957; JOSEF VON STERNBERG 1894–1969; TAY GARNETT 1894–1977; ZOLTAN KORDA 1895–1961; ROBERT SIODMAK 1900–73; WERNER HERZOG 1942–

culture clashes; displacement; exaggerated costumes and decor

From the very beginnings of cinema, the Lumière brothers sent cameramen to remote parts of the world which few people in the West had visited. However, when Hollywood studios began to be set up, the bosses felt there was no need for film crews to travel further than Los Angeles when any country on earth could be built on the back lot. Thus, the art department was able to create sets that were more Chinese than China, more Japanese than Japan, more Arab than Arabia.

It was only in the 1950s, after the postwar economic recovery, that studios sent film crews on location. This became part of the selling point of the movie with posters announcing 'Actually filmed on location'. However, it soon became redundant when location shooting became the norm rather than the exception. Nevertheless, filming on location did not prevent many films from offering a tourist's eye view and exploiting the exoticism of the country. Ernst Lubitsch once stated: 'I've been to Paris, France, but I prefer Paris Paramount.'

It was at Paramount that Josef von Sternberg was able to film Marlene Dietrich, the eternal femme fatale, in a phantasmagoric Morocco, China, Russia or Spain, conjured up by sets, make-up, wigs, costumes, light and shadow, the prime example being *Shanghai Express* (1932). Previously, another false 'von', Eric von Stroheim, had built whole Ruritanian cities on studio back lots for his cynical, erotic, exotic melodramas on decadence.

In contrast there were those directors, like Robert Flaherty, who spent two years in the Samoan islands making *Moana* (1926), and some time in India location shooting on *Elephant Boy* (1936), though much of the footage of the latter was scrapped and replaced by sequences directed in the studio by Zoltan Korda.

Some background footage was filmed on a South Sea island for John Ford's *The Hurricane* (1937), but the main part of the picture was shot on a sound stage so that the two stars, Dorothy Lamour, in a sarong, and Jon Hall, in a loincloth, never left Hollywood. Hall co-starred with Maria Montez in a series of Technicolor movies produced by Universal Pictures in the 1940s, to which the epithet 'exotic' is most frequently attached. Such films were sometimes called 'tits and sand' epics, the former mainly belonging to siren Montez and the latter referring to the recreated North African or Arabian deserts.

At the opposite extreme was Werner Herzog, who would go to any lengths to make a film in untamed regions, such as the Peruvian Andes and the Amazonian jungle for *Aguirre: Wrath of God* (1972) and *Fitzcarraldo* (1982), respectively. As the world became smaller and travel easier, exoticism in the movies became almost commonplace.

KEY WORKS

Shanghai Express, 1932, JOSEF VON STERNBERG
'It took more than one man to change my name to Shanghai Lily,' Marlene Dietrich tells her ex-lover, British army doctor Clive Brook, when they meet after five years apart. Lee Garmes won the Oscar for Best Cinematography, but it was Sternberg who was responsible for creating the lighting effects, especially the way Dietrich was lit to emphasise her mysterious beauty.

↓ **Aguirre: Wrath of God,** 1972, WERNER HERZOG
Klaus Kinski, as the megalomaniac 16th-century Spanish conquistador in the wilds of Peru, gives an enigmatic and frightening portrayal of human obsession and its consequences. Shot on location in the Peruvian rainforests, it is the topography of the landscape that dictates the action.

OTHER WORKS
Moana, 1926, FLAHERTY; **Queen Kelly,** 1928, VON STROHEIM; **Tabu,** 1931, MURNAU; **China Seas,** 1935, GARNETT; **Elephant Boy,** 1936, FLAHERTY/KORDA; **The Hurricane,** 1937, FORD; **Cobra Woman,** 1944, SIODMAK; **Fitzcarraldo,** 1982, HERZOG

 Escapism; Costume Romanticism; Emotionalism; Orientalism; Eroticism

 Naturalism; Realism; Film Noirism; Italian Neo-Realism; American Indieism

Escapism

Escapist films are those which are compelling enough to remove audiences from any consciousness of their own life and problems, drawing them intensely into an unfamiliar world far from their own. It tends to deal with uncomplex characters and simple, resolvable narrative complications.

RENÉ CLAIR 1898–1981; JEAN NEGULESCO 1900–93; ROSS HUNTER 1920–96; JACQUES DEMY 1931–90; STEVEN SPIELBERG 1946–; ROBERT ZEMECKIS 1952–

foreign settings; happy endings; linear narratives; optimism

In *Hannah and Her Sisters* (1986), Woody Allen, convinced he has a serious disease, and feeling suicidal, goes to see the Marx Brothers in *Duck Soup* (1933). He is so taken up in the comic Ruritanian world created that he leaves the cinema determined that life is still worth living. This film within a film is a prime example of the function of escapism in the movies. In another Allen picture, *The Purple Rose of Cairo* (1985), a male character in an escapist romance, literally walks off the screen into the heroine's dismal life. It demonstrates that the movies of the 1930s distorted reality by setting dangerously high expectations, but made life more bearable for the audiences during the Depression. Films took people instantly away from the breadlines in both the US and Europe.

During the Second World War, movies offered an easy, inexpensive and accessible means of escape from long working hours, austerity and the horrifying news from the front. It is, therefore, not surprising that cinema attendances tend to go up during bad periods. If one took one's knowledge of history from escapist movies, one could be forgiven for thinking that the 1930s and 1940s were affluent periods, where people spent most of their time in luxury apartments and glamorous nightclubs, typified by the films of Ernst Lubitsch, above all *Trouble in Paradise* (1932), set in a dreamlike Venice and Paris. Born during the

Depression, the musical, like no other genre, lent itself to the creation of a never-never land free from the restrictions that govern our normal daily lives.

Escapism in the movies generally comes in the form of musicals, lightweight comedies, historical romances and exotic adventures, all of which were turned out by Hollywood, 'the dream factory'. Even in the 1950s and 1960s, when American films were becoming grittier, there was a need for glossy CinemaScope entertainments like Jean Negulesco's *How To Marry a Millionaire* (1953) and *Three Coins in the Fountain* (1954), and Ross Hunter's productions featuring Doris Day.

However, many other nations had their own escapist entertainment, most of it for local consumption. Musicals and comedies were the mainstay of German cinema during the Weimar Republic, and the biggest hit under the Nazis, between the propaganda, was *Munchhausen* (1943), a lavish Agfacolor production instigated by Joseph Goebbels. In the 1930s, in the Soviet Union, Grigori Alexandrov directed four Hollywood-style musicals that pleased both Stalin and the public, while Fascist Italy produced 'white telephone' films about wealthy people, and historical pictures that looked back on the glory that was Rome.

The most widely seen escapist films have emanated from Bollywood (a conflation of Bombay, the old name for Mumbai). Rigidly formulaic Hindi-language musicals they have become increasingly popular among non-Indians. Despite the increase of realism and social awareness in the cinema, the leading box-office films throughout the world continue to be escapist ones, as witness the success of many of Spielberg's films such as *Raiders of the Lost Ark* (1981) and its sequels.

KEY WORKS

↑ **Raiders of the Lost Ark**, 1981, STEVEN SPIELBERG
Treasure hunter and archaeologist Indiana Jones (Harrison Ford) braves booby traps in an ancient temple in the Peruvian jungle in order to retrieve a Golden Idol. This throwback action-adventure, a combination of stunts and special visual effects, has no other goal than to entertain.

← **Trouble in Paradise**, 1932, ERNST LUBITSCH
The suave jewel thief Herbert Marshall is forced to choose between two beautiful amoral women, Kay Francis (left) and Miriam Hopkins. Dressed in impeccable evening clothes, the trio drifts through sumptuous art-deco sets with no hint that the film was made during the Depression. The hedonistic Lubitsch treats the audience, for a rare moment in commercial cinema, as sophisticates.

OTHER WORKS
Congress Dances, 1931, CHARELL; **Le million**, 1931, CLAIR; **Duck Soup**, 1933, MCCAREY; **Jazz Comedy**, 1934, ALEXANDROV; **The Wizard of Oz**, 1939, FLEMING; **Munchhausen**, 1943, VON BÁKY; **How To Marry a Millionaire**, 1953, NEGULESCO; **Three Coins in the Fountain**, 1954, NEGULESCO; **The Umbrellas of Cherbourg**, 1964, DEMY; **Romancing the Stone**, 1984, ZEMEKIS; **The Purple Rose of Cairo**, 1985, ALLEN

 Illusionism; Exoticism; Costume Romanticism; Utopianism; Musicalism

 Anti-Militarism; Naturalism; Realism; Dystopianism; Dogmetism

Animation encompasses many styles, themes and techniques. From the simplest hand drawing to computer-created images, it has always tried to appeal to the widest possible age range, though children have been the main target.

WINSOR MCCAY 1871–1934; **PAT SULLIVAN** 1887–1933; **WALT DISNEY** 1901–66; **TEX AVERY** 1908–80; **KAREL ZEMAN** 1910–89; **WILLIAM HANNA** 1910–2001; **JOE BARBERA** 1911–2006; **JIRÍ TRNKA** 1912–69; **CHUCK JONES** 1912–2002; **HAYAO MIYAZAKI** 1941–; **JOHN LASSETER** 1957–; **NICK PARK** 1958–

anthropomorphism; family targeted; rhythmic; humour

Devices to give drawings the illusion of movement were in use by the middle of the 19th century, long before the invention of cinema. Cartoonism truly began in 1908 when stop-motion photography was invented.

The process involves photographing drawings, puppets or inanimate objects frame by frame. When the frames are projected onto the screen at the standard speed of 24 frames a second, the subjects seem to move. In cartoons, most of the camera techniques used for live performers, such as cutting to different angles and tracking shots, are drawn.

In 1909, Winsor McCay, an American cartoonist, created *Gertie the Dinosaur* using simple line drawing. It was the first animated cartoon to be shown as part of a theatrical programme in the US. The first cartoon production units emerged between 1919 and 1920 and turned out one-reel films about 10 minutes long. This was possible due to the labour-saving method of cel animation, which allows the tracing of moving parts of characters on celluloid (or acetate) sheets without having to redraw the entire character and background for every frame of film. Perspective and depth were achieved through a multiplane camera which created realistic effects through its greater capacity for movement. In the 1920s, Pat Sullivan's Felix the Cat reigned supreme until Mickey Mouse came along.

KEY WORKS

← **Snow White and the Seven Dwarfs,** WALT DISNEY, 1937 Disney's free adaptation of the Grimm Brothers story tells of how the lovely Snow White, having fled her wicked stepmother, takes refuge in the forest home of seven dwarfs, whose names were chosen by a public poll. Four years in the making, at a cost $1.5 million, the first cartoon feature in three-strip Technicolor grossed over $8 million on its initial US release.

Mickey starred in Walt Disney's *Steamboat Willie* (1928). The first sound cartoon, it demonstrated the force of music as an element in the film's structure and visual rhythm. From 1928, cartoon characters such as Max and Dave Fleisher's Betty Boop, and Disney's Mickey Mouse and Donald Duck became as famous as film stars. Disney's studio streamlined cartoon production, consolidating its position with animated features such as *Snow White and the Seven Dwarfs* (1937) and *Fantasia* (1940), the first film to use stereo sound commercially.

While America was developing animation, other countries were experimenting with the genre. In Canada, Norman McLaren used many techniques such as drawing directly on film, mixing live action and drawings, and pixillation (the use of a stop-frame camera to speed up and distort movement.) In Czechoslovakia, Jirí Trnka, Karel Zeman and Jan Švankmajer experimented with animated models and drawings, mixing it with live action. British Nick Park's manipulation of clay models ('claymation'), particularly the characters of Wallace and Gromit – a man and his inseparable dog – became huge successes.

A new golden age dawned at the end of the 20th century with the introduction of computer-generated technology. *Toy Story* (1995) was the first cartoon feature to be completely computer generated. There was a huge rise in the popularity of Japanese anime or manga films, and cartoons specifically for adults, containing recognisable human beings, such as *The Triplets of Belleville Rendezvous* (France, 2003), *Persepolis* (France, 2007) and *Waltz with Bashir* (Israel, 2008). All of this justified the creation of an Oscar for the Best Animated Feature in 2001.

↑ **Toy Story,** 1995, JOHN LASSETER
The buddy-buddy heroes in the area of a child's bedroom are the lanky cowboy Woody (voiced by Tom Hanks) and Buzz Lightyear (Tim Allen), a macho space-ranger. The first computer-animated feature lends the characters and the space they occupy a three-dimensional reality. It also has breakneck pacing in the action sequences.

OTHER WORKS
Gertie the Dinosaur, 1909, MCCAY; **The Adventures of Prince Achmed,** 1926, REINIGER; **Steamboat Willie,** 1928, DISNEY; **Fantasia** (1940), ALGAR/ARMSTRONG; **King-Size Canary,** 1947, AVERY; **The Wrong Trousers,** 1993, NICK PARK; **Spirited Away,** 2001, MIYAZAKI; **Shrek,** 2001, ADAMSON/JENSON; **The Triplets of Belleville,** 2003, CHOMET; **Persepolis,** 2007, PARONNAUD/SATRAPI; **Waltz with Bashir,** 2008, FOLMAN

 Illusionism; Surrealism; Escapism; Musicalism; FX-ism

 Athleticism; Documentarism; Realism; Film Noirism; Minimalism

Poetic realism is used to describe a group of French films made between 1934 and 1940 that combined realism with a lyrical style of filmmaking. The atmosphere, created by impressionistic lighting and decor, was generally dark and fatalistic, prefiguring American film noir.

JACQUES FEYDER 1887–1948; JEAN RENOIR 1894–1979; JULIEN DUVIVIER 1896–1967; JACQUES PRÉVERT 1900–77; JEAN GABIN 1904–76; PIERRE CHENAL 1904–90; ALEXANDRE TRAUNER 1906–93; MARCEL CARNÉ 1909–96

artificial atmospheric sets; marginalised characters; moody sensitivity; suggestive symbolism; working-class milieu

With its roots in realist 19th-century literature, poetic realism reflected the low morale of France during the immediate pre-Second World War years. Set mostly in working-class milieu, the films had downbeat story lines, often focusing on marginalised characters seeking unattainable love. Two of the first were Jean Renoir's *La nuit du carrefour (Night at the Crossroads,* 1932), based on an Inspector Maigret story by Georges Simenon, and Jacques Feyder's *Le grand jeu* (1934). Though they differed in style, the two films shared an absurdist view of the world. Renoir lends the former, with its inexplicable events and motives, a dark, decadent and hallucinatory aspect. Feyder's film, with exotic set designs by Lazare Meerson, takes place in Morocco where a legionnaire falls for a cabaret singer who resembles the society woman he has tried to forget.

One of the assistant directors on the film was Marcel Carné who, with the poet Jacques Prévert, went on to create two of

the most archetypal poetic realist films, *Le quai des brumes* (*Port of Shadows*, 1938) and *Le jour se lève* (*Daybreak*, 1939), both dominated by the powerful brooding presence of Jean Gabin, a quintessential loner who combined French working-class masculinity with the destiny of a tragic hero. Described by the critic André Bazin as 'Oedipus in a cloth cap', he epitomised the poetic realist protagonist.

In *Le quai des brumes* he is an army deserter trying to gain some happiness in a fog-bound port (superb sets by Alexandre Trauner), and in the latter he is a worker wanted for a *crime passionnel* who has barricaded himself in his small dark tenement room as the police and crowds wait below.

Gabin's moody persona was also an essential element in Julien Duvivier's *Pépé Le Moko* (1936) in which he is a jewel thief hiding in the Algerian Casbah who is caught when he is tempted out by the love of a beautiful Parisienne; and reaches tragic stature as the train driver forced to murder his lover's husband in Renoir's *La bête humaine* (*The Human Beast*, 1938), updated from Émile Zola's 1890 novel to the 1930s, and combining the hopes of the Popular Front (the alliance of left-wing movements that won the May 1936 elections) and the gloom of the approaching war.

Pierre Chenal's *Crime and Punishment* (1935) and *Le dernier tournant* (*The Last Bend*, 1939) managed to make writers Dostoevsky and James M Cain (*The Postman Always Rings Twice*), respectively, express the Zeitgeist. The characteristic mood of romantic despair infused Carné's *Hôtel du Nord* (1938), in which Arletty, standing on the bridge over the Canal Saint-Martin and looking at her dismal surroundings, famously cries 'Atmosphère', atmosphere!', a line that came to typify poetic realism.

KEY WORKS

 Le quai des brumes (Port of Shadows),
1938, MARCEL CARNÉ
The slant-eyed 18-year-old Michèle Morgan, in a trench coat and beret, together with the doomed Jean Gabin as an army deserter, who has fled to a sombre fog-bound Le Havre, trying to grab some happiness, are the quintessential images associated with the world-weariness prevalent in pre-Second World War France.

 Le grand jeu, 1934, JACQUES FEYDER
The foreign legionnaire (Pierre Richard-Willm) has his fortune told by the proprietress (Françoise Rosay, Feyder's wife) of a cheap hotel in Morocco. Her cards foretell a brave death in his next campaign. The title refers to the practice of giving the whole story (*Le grand jeu*) of the cards no matter how horrible. The film was one of the first French films to define the characteristic mood of romantic despair.

OTHER WORKS
La nuit du carrefour (Night at the Crossroads), 1932, RENOIR; Crime and Punishment, 1935, CHENAL; Pépé Le Moko, 1936, DUVIVIER; La bête humaine (The Human Beast), 1938, RENOIR; Hôtel du Nord, 1938, Le jour se lève (Daybreak), 1939, CARNÉ; Le dernier tournant (The Last Bend), 1939, CHENAL;

Naturalism; Realism; Film Noirism; Italian Neo-Realism; Eroticism

Illusionism; Monumentalism; Socialist Realism; Escapism; Utopianism

Costume Romanticism

The aim of the costume drama is to attract an audience's attention as much to the period dresses and decor as to the narrative of the film. The settings of the films generally date from the end of the Renaissance when dress was becoming more colourful.

CLARENCE BROWN 1890–1987; ERNST LUBITSCH 1892–1947; ALEXANDER KORDA 1893–1956; SERGEI EISENSTEIN 1898–1948; MAX OPHÜLS 1902–57; LUCHINO VISCONTI 1906–76; DAVID LEAN 1908–91; JAMES IVORY 1928–; BERNARDO BERTOLUCCI 1940–

accurate historical backgrounds; lavish costumes and settings; romantic plots

Costume Romanticism

Most of the classic romantic costume dramas or period pieces, typified by lavish costumes and design, derive from literary sources. The costume drama tends to concentrate on the fashionable wealthy, capturing only one aspect of a particular era in meticulous, sometimes exaggerated, detail. The plots often merge fictional

KEY WORKS

↓ Gone with the Wind, 1939, VICTOR FLEMING
The wilful minx Scarlett O' Hara (Vivien Leigh) does the Virginia reel at the Atlanta charity ball with the roguish Rhett Butler (Clark Gable). The scene, one of the many spectacular set-pieces that evoke the Old South, has an element of shock because Scarlett, in black, is so recently widowed. As she says: 'I'm too young to be a widow.'

characters with real historical figures and events.

Many of the earliest examples were rather static reconstructions until Ernst Lubitsch livened up the genre in Germany with a few historical romances such as *Madame DuBarry* (1919) and *Anna Boleyn* (1920). Clarence Brown directed seven pictures with Greta Garbo, mostly glossy romances in plush surroundings. But it was not until the first feature film in colour, Rouben Mamoulian's *Becky Sharp* (1935), that costume romanticism came into its own. Technicolor and costume drama were made for each other, the peak being reached with *Gone With the Wind* (1939).

Nevertheless, there were still popular period romances in black and white, such as the Gainsborough Pictures melodramas in England, the best being *The Wicked Lady* (1945) starring Margaret Lockwood and James Mason. In France, in the 1950s, Max Ophüls sublimely summoned up 19th-century Vienna and the Second Empire, while Claude Autant-Lara successfully adapted Stendhal, Maupassant and Dostoevsky to the screen. It was against the latter type of period film that the French *Nouvelle Vague* (New Wave) reacted, though François Truffaut, Éric Rohmer and Jacques Rivette subsequently all made less academic costume dramas.

In Italy, former neo-realists Luchino Visconti and Roberto Rossellini directed some of the most superb and persuasive costume dramas. Rossellini approached the subject of *The Rise to Power of Louis XIV* (1966) in a direct and realistic manner to reveal the man beneath the regal wig. At first we see the king gaining in authority as he gets dressed in the morning, and at the end the little king is exposed when divested of his robes. Visconti reached the artistic peak in the genre with the lush operatic spectacle of *Senso* (1954) and *The Leopard* (1963), a gorgeous evocation of the dying aristocratic world during the Risorgimento, both of which benefit from stunning colour photography.

In England, American-born James Ivory, with his own company set up with Indian producer Ismail Merchant, made refined and beautifully designed adaptations of novels by Henry James and EM Forster, and opened up a resurgence of the interest in Jane Austen's novels, most of which were filmed in the 1990s and early 21st century. Martin Scorsese (*The Age of Innocence*, 1993) and Stanley Kubrick (*Barry Lyndon*, 1975), both ventured uncharacteristically, but triumphantly, into the genre.

→ **The Leopard,** 1963, LUCHINO VISCONTI
The dashing young revolutionary Tancredi (Alain Delon) with his wife (Claudia Cardinale) at the climactic ball, a superb set-piece that takes up more than 40 minutes of screen time. It is the marriage of his penniless nephew to the daughter of a merchant that causes the Prince of Salina (Burt Lancaster) to reflect sadly on the death of the aristocratic world in this gorgeous evocation of an era.

OTHER WORKS
Madame DuBarry, 1919, LUBITSCH; **Anna Boleyn,** 1920, LUBITSCH; **Becky Sharp,** 1935, MAMOULIAN; **Ivan the Terrible (Parts I and II),** 1944, 1946, EISENSTEIN; **The Wicked Lady,** 1945, ARLISS; **Senso,** 1954, VISCONTI; **Lola Montès,** 1955, OPHÜLS; **The Rise to Power of Louis XIV,** 1966, ROSSELLINI; **Barry Lyndon,** 1975, KUBRICK ; **The Draughtsman's Contract,** 1982, GREENAWAY; **The Last Emperor,** 1987, BERTOLUCCI; **Dangerous Liaisons,** 1988, FREARS; **The Age of Innocence,** 1993, SCORSESE; **La reine Margot,** 1994, CHÉREAU

Exoticism; Escapism; Emotionalism; Biographism; Classicism

Avant-Gardism; Film Noirism; Italian Neo-Realism; New Wavism; American Indieism

🕐 The anti-war film emerged after the desolation of the First World War. However, there is often a thin line drawn between the drama, adventure and heroics that war provides and the condemnation of it in cinema.

🕐 **JOHN FORD** 1894–1973; **JEAN RENOIR** 1894–1979; **LEWIS MILESTONE** 1895–1980; **HOWARD HAWKS** 1896–1977; **ABEL GANCE** 1889–1981; **SAM FULLER** 1912–97; **KON ICHIKAWA** 1915–2008; **ANDRZEJ WAJDA** 1926–

🕐 evenhandedness; realism; suffering; violence

⚫ Anti-militarist films have rarely been made during wars, when there is a tendency to stir up popular support for the cause. Films that demonstrate that there are no winners in such a conflict have been produced when the wars are distant enough to avoid nationalism and to be able to censure war in general. Anti-war films demonstrate the brutality of war in a more realistic manner as well as being more complex in their portrayal of the combatants. Satire has also been an effective way to puncture inflated ideas of war.

Of all the wars, the First World War is the most emblematic. As no other war seemed as futile, it was easier to make convincing anti-war statements. Yet, paradoxically,

great films on the subject have been few and far between since Jean Renoir's *La grande illusion* (1937), a paradigm for all subsequent films on the subject. Only Stanley Kubrick's *Paths of Glory* (1957) came close.

Abel Gance's *J'accuse* (1919), described by the director as 'a human cry against the bellicose din of armies', depicted death, delusion and insanity in the trenches. Made in Hollywood, Lewis Milestone's *All Quiet on the Western Front* (1930) was seen from the German perspective. Particularly effective were the tracking shots of soldiers attacking the enemy lines and the counter-attacks with death on both sides. So realistic were these sequences that they have often been used in documentary films of the war. In the same year, in Germany itself, GW Pabst's *Westfront 1918* revealed the horror of life in the trenches. But as the memories of the war and the mood of anti-militarism that marked these films began to fade, so the subject became less popular.

As a result, although *La grande illusion* came out of a tradition of anti-war films, Jean Renoir's masterpiece shows nothing of 'war-is-hell' fighting; neither does it resort to any rhetoric or sentimental pleas for universal brotherhood. The Russian Sergei Bondarchuk's remarkable eight-hour *War and Peace* (1966) could be considered as anti-militarism on an epic scale.

Not surprisingly, the countries that suffered the most deaths during the Second World War – Russia, Poland and Japan – have delivered the most devastating anti-militarist films, notably Elem Klimov's *Come and See* (1985), Andrzej Wajda's war trilogy (*A Generation,* 1954, *Kanal*, 1957, *Ashes and Diamonds*, 1958) and Kon Ichikawa's *The Burmese Harp* (1956) and *Fires on the Plain* (1959).

In most cases some time is needed to elapse after hostilities before a film directly

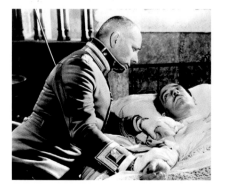

The Big Red One, 1980, SAM FULLER
Lee Marvin (right) is the war-weary sergeant who acts in loco parentis to a rifle squad of rookies, including Mark Hamill (left) at the end of the Second World War. Hamill, a semi-pacifist, changes his views on liberating a concentration camp. The power of Fuller's direction is in its reduction of war to its essentials.

denouncing a war can be broached. Perhaps the war films of John Ford, Howard Hawks and Sam Fuller, whose movies, such as *The Big Red One* (1980), came out of his own war experiences, are the most ambivalent. The US took several years to approach the Vietnam War critically. With *Apocalypse Now* (1979), Francis Ford Coppola succeeded in his desire to 'give its audience a sense of the horror, the madness, the sensuousness and the dilemma of the Vietnam War'.

KEY WORKS

La grande illusion, 1937, JEAN RENOIR
Captain von Rauffenstein (Eric von Stroheim) at the bedside of the dying Captain de Boeldieu (Pierre Fresnay), whom he has had to shoot out of duty, despite sympathies with his fellow aristocrat, when the latter attempts to escape the prisoner-of-war fortress. Boeldieu says: 'For a common man it's terrible to die in war. For you and me, it's a good solution.'

OTHER WORKS

Westfront 1918, 1930, PABST; **A Generation**, 1954 WAJDA; **Kanal**, 1957 WAJDA; **Ashes and Diamonds**, 1958, WAJDA; **J'accuse**, 1919, GANCE; **All Quiet on the Western Front**, 1930, MILESTONE; **The Burmese Harp**, 1956, ICHIKAWA; **Paths of Glory**, 1957, KUBRICK; **Fires on the Plain**, 1959, ICHIKAWA; **War and Peace**, 1966, BONDARCHUK; **Oh! What a Lovely War**, 1969, ATTENBOROUGH; **Apocalypse Now**, 1979, COPPOLA; **Come and See**, 1985, KLIMOV; **Das Boot**, 1981, PETERSEN; **Flags of Our Fathers**, 2006, EASTWOOD; **Letters from Iwo Jima**, 2006, EASTWOOD

 Documentarism; Propagandism; Realism; Liberalism; Revisionism

 Escapism; Costume Romanticism; Racialism; Utopianism; Westernism

THE WAR YEARS
1939–45

🕐 Part of film's effectiveness in documentary form came from the widely held idea that the camera cannot lie. But overt propaganda has been used as much in fictional drama to convey a 'message'.

◐ ALEXANDER DOVZHENKO 1894–1956; GW PABST 1885–1967; SERGEI EISENSTEIN 1898–1948; VEIT HARLAN 1899–1964; LENI RIEFENSTAHL 1902–2003; MICHAEL POWELL 1905–90; PARE LORENTZ 1905–92; HUMPHREY JENNINGS 1907–50)

◔ bold strokes; documentary style; lack of complexity; message and narrative aligned

● Most feature films have some sort of message to convey to the viewer, but the term 'propagandism' can only be applied to such films when their entertainment value functions almost exclusively as a vehicle for the message. Propaganda films came of age during the First World War when every major belligerent power commissioned official films showing the enemy in an unfavourable light. Apart from newsreels, commercial films were found to have great propagandistic value, for example DW Griffiths' *Hearts of the World* (1918), in which the Germans are presented as brutes. In the Soviet Union, Lenin realised that film was the most important of all the arts because it could educate the masses,

many of whom were illiterate, to support Bolshevik aims. The agit-trains toured the vast country with Dziga Vertov's *Kino-Pravda* (literally, Cinematic Truth) newsreels. Almost all of the great silent Soviet films, such as those by Sergei Eisenstein and Alexander Dovzhenko, were made for propaganda purposes.

Between the wars, many films, principally documentaries, exposed social evils. In the UK, John Grierson produced films such as *Coal Face* and *Housing Problems* (both 1935) for the Crown Film Unit, while Pare Lorentz, Grierson's counterpart in the US, attempted to convince the public to accept President Roosevelt's New Deal, after the Depression, with *The Plow That Broke the Plains* (1936) and *The River* (1937).

In Germany, GW Pabst made *Kameradschaft* (1931), a plea for the international solidarity of workers, illustrated by German miners rescuing their French comrades trapped underground near the Franco-German border. Slatan Dudow's *Kuhle Wampe* (1932), a passionate propaganda piece on the homeless, which included ballads, was the only film that the playwright Bertolt Brecht was involved in that did not distort his intentions. All changed the following year with the coming of the Third Reich when anti-Semitic films became de rigueur, such as Veit Harlan's *Jew Suss* (1940), a travesty of Feuchtwanger's pro-Jewish novel of 1925. However, the most (in)famous Nazi propaganda film was *Triumph of the Will* (1935), Leni Riefenstahl's spectacular documentary of the 1934 Nuremberg Rally showing Hitler as a Wagnerian hero descending on the medieval town to save *Das Volk*.

During the Second World War, a stream of anti-Nazi dramas was produced by the Allies. In Britain, among Michael Powell and Emeric Pressburger's wartime fiction films, the most didactic was *49th Parallel* (1941), which contrasts fascism with Canadian democracy. The documentaries of Humphrey Jennings, about the effects of war on ordinary citizens, including *London Can Take It* (1940) and *Fires Were Started* (1943), did much to influence public opinion in America. Frank Capra, John Huston and John Ford all served with the American Office of Information, making important contributions to the war effort. During the Cold War there were only a handful of crude anti-Communist fiction films (for example, *I Was a Communist for the FBI*, 1951) and these had little effect on the liberal climate of 1960s and 1970s America.

OTHER WORKS
Hearts of the World, 1918, GRIFFITHS; The General Line, 1928, EISENSTEIN; Arsenal, 1929, DOVZHENKO; Kameradschaft, 1931, PABST; Kuhle Wampe, 1932, DUDOW; Coal Face, 1935, GRIERSON; Housing Problems, 1935, GRIERSON; The Plow That Broke the Plains, 1936, LORENTZ; Jew Suss, 1940, HARLAN; London Can Take It, 1940, JENNINGS; 49th Parallel, 1941, POWELL/PRESSBURGER; Listen to Britain, 1942, JENNINGS; I Was a Communist for the FBI, 1951, DOUGLAS

 Documentarism; Socialist Realism; Racialism; Anti-Militarism; Liberalism

 Avant-Gardism; Screwballism; Escapism; Dystopianism; Minimalism

KEY WORKS

Triumph of the Will, 1935, LENI RIEFENSTAHL
Leni Reifenstahl giving instructions to one of the more than 40 cameramen supplied to her by the Nazi Party to make this documentary on the 1934 Nuremberg rally under a title suggested by Hitler. Despite the director's later protestations that it was merely a record of a historical event and not a propaganda film, she helped shape the rally into a great mythic spectacle.

Fires Were Started, 1943, HUMPHREY JENNINGS
One of the courageous firemen of the National Fire Service during one particular day and night in the middle of the London Blitz. The film, like others by Jennings, has none of the hectoring tone of most propaganda, but was subtle, poignant and human, though made with a patriotic purpose in mind.

In 1932, in the Soviet Union, the slogan 'socialist realism' became de rigueur in all the arts. It affirmed that Soviet art must reflect Bolshevik values, be understandable and loved by the masses and, by the portrayal of fortitude and optimism, help build socialism.

VSEVOLOD PUDOVKIN 1893–1953; ALEXANDER DOVZHENKO 1894–1956; SERGEI EISENSTEIN 1898–1948; MARK DONSKOI 1901–81; LEONID TRAUBERG 1902–90; SERGEI YUTKEVICH 1904–85; GRIGORI KOZINTSEV 1905–73; JIN XIE 1923–2008

grand gestures; optimism; propaganda; stylised acting

Socialist realism, a phrase attributed to Stalin, embodied the leader's vision for the future. Every feature was required to glorify the ideals of the revolution and depict the power of the collective. Socialist realism had a dialectical antithesis – 'formalism', ie experimental or modern art.

However, this portrayal of Soviet life came at the cost of censorship and suppression of individual artistic talents.

Despite the restrictions, Sergei Eisenstein managed personal touches in his patriotic pageant *Alexander Nevsky* (1938), the costumes alone conjuring up a fantastic folk tale. The staging of the battles in the film influenced those in non-socialist realist films.

When Stalin praised *Chapayev* (1934), it became the model for subsequent non-socialist realist films such as Laurence Olivier's *Henry V* (1944) and Orson Welles's *Chimes At Midnight* (1965). It followed the exploits of the eponymous Red Army commander fighting against Czech and Kolchak forces during the civil war of 1919. This led to other hagiographic films portraying heroes of socialism, including several on Lenin.

Baltic Deputy (1937), which ably balanced propaganda, action, humour and pathos,

showed how a distinguished Russian scientist (played by the imposing Nikolai Cherkassov), despite ostracism by his colleagues, joined the Bolsheviks in 1918 and became a hero of the revolution.

Though sticking to the party line, two trilogies, known as *The Maxim Trilogy* (1935–9) and *The Gorky Trilogy* (1938–40), were studies of flesh-and-blood unromanticised individuals caught up in the pre-revolutionary struggle against the exploitation of workers and peasants.

Many of the great directors of the silent era, like Vsevolod Pudovkin, found it difficult to adapt to socialist realism and fell by the wayside. Nevertheless, Alexander Dovzhenko was able to bring some of the lyricism of his earlier pastoral silent films to bear on more industrial subjects such as *Aerograd* (1935), about the construction of a new city in Siberia. When Stalin asked Dovzhenko to come up with a 'Ukrainian *Chapayev* ', the director delivered *Shchors* (1939), a vivid, heroic epic of pro-Bolshevik Ukrainian partisans who liberated Kiev from the Germans in 1918.

Other countries in the Soviet bloc were also forced to make propaganda films in a similar style during the Stalinist period. The films of the People's Republic of China also operated under strict socialist realist guidelines, many of them revised versions of classic Peking operas such as *The Red Detachment of Women* (1960). The film revealed Jin Xie's vivid sense of colour, composition and inventive camera angles, as did the finely crafted *Two Stage Sisters* (1965).

Gradually, with relative liberalisation in the Communist countries, socialist realism was replaced by a more humanistic and realistic cinema.

KEY WORKS

↑ **Shchors,** 1939, ALEXANDER DOVZHENKO, YULIYA SOLNTSEVA
A soldier in the regiment of pro-Bolshevik Ukranian partisans celebrates the liberation of Kiev from the Germans in 1918 under the leadership of the young Nikolai Shchors. The film contains some of the poetic imagery for which Dovzhenko was renowned, and also demonstrated his ability to use characters to embody ideas without taking away their humanity.

← **Alexander Nevsky,** 1938, SERGEI EISENSTEIN
Prince Alexander Nevsky (Nikolai Cherkasov, centre) has formed a people's army to drive brutal Teutonic invaders from the soil of Holy Russia in 1242. Although Cherkasov has the charisma and stature to hold the film together, Nevsky is presented as a conqueror striking heroic poses at the centre of a grandiloquent historical fresco.

OTHER WORKS

Golden Mountains, 1931, YUTKEVICH; **The Deserter,** 1933, PUDOVKIN; **Chapayev,** 1934, VASILYEV/VASILYEV; **Aerograd,** 1935, DOVZHENKO; **Baltic Deputy,** 1937, ZHARKI/HEIFITS; **The Maxim Trilogy: The Youth of Maxim,** 1935, **The Return of Maxim,** 1937, **The Vyborg Side,** 1939, KOZINTSEV/TRAUBERG; **The Gorky Trilogy: The Childhood of Maxim Gorky,** 1938, **My Apprenticeship,** 1939, **My Universities,** 1940, DONSKOI; **The Red Detachment of Women,** 1960, XIE; **Two Stage Sisters,** 1965, XIE

 Monumentalism; Constructivism; Propagandism; Biographism; Utopianism

 Avant-Gardism; Surrealism; Anti-Militarism; Revisionism

Racialism exists in films of two types: those that promote racialism and those that are unwittingly racist. Because the major part of the history of Hollywood has always lagged behind wider social advances, the latter type has been more prevalent .

DW GRIFFITH 1875–1948; **CECIL B DEMILLE** (1881–1959; **JOHN FORD** 1894–1973; **VEIT HARLAN** 1899–1964; **WALT DISNEY** 1901–66

propaganda; reductionism; simplification; stereotypes

Because Hollywood studios were part of an ideological superstructure determined by the capitalist economic system and, since their inception, they have projected a largely conservative white middle-class view of the world, it is not surprising that racism, unwitting or otherwise, was reflected in films. African Americans and Native Americans suffered most from stereotyping.

Blacks were mainly called upon to play stock, wide-eyed cowards or 'uncles' and 'mammies' as well as ignoble savages such as in the *Tarzan* movies of the 1930s and 1940s. There was also the tradition of whites blacking up, as seen in the historic first sound feature, *The Jazz Singer* (1927).

'Red Indians' in westerns such as John Ford's *Drums Along the Mohawk* (1939) and Cecil B DeMille's *Unconquered* (1947) were portrayed as bloodthirsty, depraved rapists and murderers. Apart from the 'savages' in Ford's *Stagecoach* (1939), there is also the archetypal dumb Mexican. When they were not cast as idiots in sombreros, Mexicans were mean, moustachioed bandits. There were the expendable Arabs in colonial adventures like *Beau Geste* (1939), and the multitude of wily Asians exemplified by the *Fu Manchu* films, with white actors

yellowing-up. Even sympathetic portrayals of Asians, such as Richard Barthelmess in *Broken Blossoms* (1919), subtitled *The Yellow Man and the Girl*, and Katharine Hepburn in *Dragon Seed* (1944), are now seen as demeaning.

Jews were spared the worst of these indignities (possibly because they were at least well represented within the industry's higher echelons), though their visibility was still limited at best. Jews as Jews were more or less unseen in Hollywood movies where stars such as Tony Curtis, Kirk Douglas and Jerry Lewis hid their origins behind Anglo-Saxon names.

The ground-breaking *The Birth of a Nation* (1915), in which the hero forms the Ku Klux Klan, and a black man pursues a white virgin who kills herself rather than succumb to his attentions was, even at that period, considered by many to be racially offensive.

During the two world wars it was considered justified to grossly caricature the Germans and the Japanese, just as they were doing the same with Americans and the British. Nazi Germany, of course, made anti-Semitic propaganda films, the most celebrated being Veit Harlan's *Jew Suss* (1940).

Gradually, in the 1950s, Hollywood began to have a less passive acceptance of the mores of the dominant film culture, and had a wider critical perspective in relation to misrepresentation of races in the cinema. However, Arabs continue to be the most maligned of all races in Western movies, where they are seen as stock villains or comic relief, which a few films, like *Lawrence of Arabia* (1962), tried to dispel. Yet, after the 11 September attacks, Arabs and terrorism have been even more closely linked in films than was previously the case.

KEY WORKS

↑ Jew Suss, 1940, VEIT HARLAN
In the 18th century, financial adviser Süss Openheimer (Ferdinand Marian) uses evil methods to gain power for himself and his people. Made with the personal encouragement of Josef Goebbels, the film, though well made by Harlan, is a travesty of Feuchtwanger's pro-Jewish novel of 1925.

← The Birth of a Nation, 1915, DW GRIFFITH
The scene depicts the 'renegade Negro', Gus, played by white actor Walter Long in black face, about to be lynched by the Ku Klux Klan. Griffith allows public history to give way to private myth by showing the hero forming the Klan to restore law and order to the South.

OTHER WORKS
Broken Blossoms, 1919, GRIFFITH; The Jazz Singer, 1927, CROSLAND; Beau Geste, 1939, WELLMAN; Drums Along the Mohawk, 1939, FORD; Gone With The Wind, 1939, FLEMING; Stagecoach, 1939, FORD; The Eternal Jew, 1940, FRITZ HIPPLER; Dragon Seed, 1944, BUCQUET/CONWAY; Song of the South, 1946, DISNEY; Unconquered, 1947, DEMILLE

 Hollywood Studioism; Exoticism; Propagandism; Socialist Realism; Westernism

 Naturalism; Realism; Liberalism; Revisionism; American Indieism

Naturalism in the cinema derives from the school of 19th-century fiction that showed characters as victims of natural forces. This naturalistic principle could be summed up by the title of Émile Zola's 1890 novel *La bête humaine* (*The Human Beast*), adapted by Jean Renoir for his 1938 film.

FRITZ LANG 1890–1976; JEAN RENOIR 1894–1979; JEAN GRÉMILLON 1901–59; MARCEL CARNÉ 1909–96; JOHN CASSAVETES 1929–89; MIKE LEIGH 1943–

crime and punishment; mainly working-class characters; natural forces; pessimism; realism

Naturalism, the 19th-century philosophy which believed that the individual's fate is primarily determined not by free will but by heredity and environment, was associated with the novels of Émile Zola and American writers Frank Norris and Theodore Dreiser, in turn heavily influenced by Zola. Naturalistic film adaptations, faithful to the spirit of these novelists, share a pessimistic viewpoint with poetic realism, though they tend to be more realistic than poetic. Whereas realism seeks to depict life as it really is, naturalism attempts to determine 'scientifically' the

underlying forces influencing the actions of its characters, often caught up in inextricably difficult situations. Murder, especially *crime passionnel*, plays an important part in many of the plots.

Eric von Stroheim's *Greed* (1924), a morality tale about the dehumanising influence of money, was filmed almost entirely on location, often at the exact settings of Norris' novel *McTeague* (1899). Von Stroheim wanted to make it with complete fidelity, 'picturising' each sentence. In its original 10-hour version, it remains the greatest film never seen, but even in its 150-minute version it remains a naturalistic masterpiece.

Jean Renoir, who felt an affinity with the tenets of naturalism, adapted Zola twice in *Nana* (1926) and *La bête humaine* (*The Human Beast*, 1938), and several of his other films, such as *La chienne* (1931) and *Toni* (1935), are naturalistic in theme and style. Fritz Lang, many of whose Hollywood films were dark fatalistic tales of murder, revenge and seduction, remade *La chienne* as *Scarlet Street* (1945) and *La bête humaine* as *Human Desire* (1954). Marcel Carné, more associated with poetic realism, updated *Thérèse Raquin* (1953), Zola's novel of destructive sensual passion, redolent with brooding atmosphere.

Jean Grémillon's *Lumière d'été* (*Summer Light*, 1943) is a melancholy allegory of characters living on the edge of a figurative and literal abyss, while *Remorques* (*Stormy Waters*, 1941) and *Gueule d'amour* (*Lover Boy*, 1937), perceptive studies of passion and the nature of fidelity, starred Jean Gabin, perfect as a doomed lover. Although Luchino Visconti's *Ossessione* (1943) was the first film to be labelled neo-realist, it belongs, with its illicit affair and murder leading to inevitable tragedy, to the naturalist tradition.

Though very different in style and plots from the French dramas of the 1930s and 1940s, John Cassavetes' explorations of characters, generally going through mid-life emotional crises, have the attributes of naturalism. Using rather similar improvisational techniques to Cassavetes, Mike Leigh roots his naturalistic social critiques in the idiosyncrasies of his characters who echo American author Henry David Thoreau's remark that 'most people lead lives of quiet desperation'.

KEY WORKS

Greed, 1924, ERIC VON STROHEIM
A personification of the film's title, in a performance of harrowing intensity, ZaSu Pitts as a woman obsessed with money counts her gold coins won in a huge lottery, none of which she will spend even though she and her husband are in dire straits. She is eventually murdered for the money she hoards.

↑ La bête humaine (The Human Beast), 1938, JEAN RENOIR
Engine driver Jacques Lantier (Jean Gabin) falls in love with the stationmaster's wife Séverine (sex-kittenish Simone Simon), a fateful affair that leads to murder and suicide. Gabin's other love in the film is for La Lison, his locomotive which is filmed as a mechanical Beauty driven by a human Beast.

OTHER WORKS

Nana, 1926, La chienne, 1931, Toni, 1935, RENOIR; Remorques (Stormy Waters), 1941, Lumière d'été (Summer Light), 1943, GRÉMILLON; Ossessione, 1943, VISCONTI; Scarlet Street, 1945, LANG; Thérèse Raquin, 1953, CARNÉ; Human Desire, 1954, LANG; This Sporting Life, 1963, ANDERSON; A Woman Under the Influence, 1974, CASSAVETES; My American Uncle, 1980, RESNAIS; Germinal, 1993, BERRI; Secrets and Lies, 1996, LEIGH

 Expressionism; Poetic Realism; Realism; Film Noirism; Italian Neo-Realism

 Illusionism; Surrealism; Escapism; Socialist Realism; Utopianism

Realism is a convenient label that has been attached to a multitude of films, all of which make claim to their verisimilitude to real life. More particularly, it refers to films that, like their 19th-century literary predecessors, emphasise description and relish the details of everyday life.

JEAN RENOIR 1894–1979; JEAN VIGO 1905–34; SATYAJIT RAY 1921–92; MAURICE PIALAT 1925–2003; KEN LOACH 1936–; ABBAS KIAROSTAMI 1940–; JEAN-PIERRE DARDENNE 1951–; LUC DARDENNE 1954–; JAFAR PANAHI 1960–

deep focus; direct sound; everyday life; non-stars; ordinary people

Realist films distance themselves from the conventional codes of narration as typified by Hollywood. According to the Italian screenwriter Cesare Zavattini, 'reality in American films is unnaturally filtered'. Realism is concerned with the lives of ordinary, usually working-class people, those marginalised by mainstream cinema

and society. In a sense this makes it a political cinema, though not overtly so. However, unlike the documentary, realism does not claim to be an exact representation of reality but an approach to it. For example, Gillo Pontecorvo achieved a realistic quality in *The Battle of Algiers* (1966), coming closer to the truth and complexities of the French-Algerian War than any documentary. Realist films reject period pieces in order to concentrate on the actions of the contemporary world.

For André Bazin it was a cinema whose chief elements were the long take, deep focus, limited editing and, when possible, the use of non-professional or relatively unknown actors. Jean Vigo believed in a social cinema that would reject both Hollywood and the avant-garde, and instead be 'continuously replenished by reality'. Everyday life is filled with magical moments in Vigo's *L'Atalante* (1934), a masterpiece of realistic cinema, a simple story of a young barge captain who takes his bride to live on

his boat that plies the canals around Paris.

The history of cinema began with the realism of the films of Auguste and Louis Lumière, such as workers leaving the factory, men playing cards, a family having breakfast, a barge on a river. This 'realist tendency', as critic Siegfried Kracauer called it, reappeared in its truest form in the works of Jean Renoir in the 1930s. Typically, in *Boudu Saved from Drowning* (1932), Renoir took his camera and sound equipment out on location, filming the people in the streets, a marching band, and weekend trippers picnicking at the riverside creating a real, habitable world. In *The Rules of the Game* (1939), Renoir applied realism to the upper classes, though the servants were treated with equal importance, mainly through the use of depth of field, which kept them in focus.

It was Renoir who inspired Satyajit Ray to embark on *The Apu Trilogy* (1955–9), which entirely altered notions of Indian cinema. In fact, it was Third World cinema, mainly out of necessity, that developed a realist cinema, and especially the vibrant Iranian films of the 1990s. In the UK, Ken Loach is the most ardent practitioner of realism, as are the Dardenne brothers in Belgium, effectively employing the hand-held camera, relatively unknown actors and natural lighting. Maurice Pialat's intense emotional authenticity, a master of laying bare reality, inspired a generation of 1990s French filmmakers.

↑ The Apu Trilogy (Pather Panchali, The Unvanquished, The World of Apu), 1955, 1956, 1959, SATYAJIT RAY
In *Pather Panchali*, Karuna Banerjee (left) as the mother, and Uma Das Gupta, the daughter, make a fuss of Subir Banerjee as Apu, whose adventures the trilogy follows from his birth into his 30s. Shot over eight years, entirely in natural surroundings, with non-professional actors, in the regional language of Bengali, the film led to new conventions of realism in Indian cinema.

OTHER WORKS
L'Atalante, 1934, VIGO; The Rules of the Game, 1939, RENOIR; The Battle of Algiers, 1966, PONTECORVO; Loulou, 1980, PIALAT; Naked, 1993, LEIGH; The Mirror, 1997, PANAHI; Taste of Cherry, 1997, KIAROSTAMI; Rosetta, 1999, DARDENNE/DARDENNE; Sweet Sixteen, 2003, LOACH

KEY WORKS
Boudu Saved from Drowning, 1932, JEAN RENOIR
As the scruffy tramp Boudu, Michel Simon gives one of the greatest of screen performances. Having been rescued by a benign bourgeois bookseller from drowning himself in the Seine, Boudu sets about seducing his rescuer's wife (Marcelle Hainia, right) and the maid. 'One should only help those of one's own class,' the bookseller concludes.

 Documentarism; Poetic Realism; Naturalism; Italian Neo-Realism; Minimalism

 Illusionism; Surrealism; Escapism; Socialist Realism; Musicalism

Film noir is a term that French critics applied to the dark, doom-laden, black-and-white Hollywood crime movies of the 1940s that were seen in French cinemas for the first time only after the Second World War. Film noir was thought to reflect postwar anxiety and cynicism.

FRITZ LANG 1890–1976; HOWARD HAWKS 1896–1977; ROBERT SIODMAK 1900–73; OTTO PREMINGER 1905–86; JOHN HUSTON 1906–87; BILLY WILDER 1906–2002; HENRI-GEORGES CLOUZOT 1907–77

chiaroscuro; claustrophobic; low-key lighting; nihilism; off-centre angles;

Film noir is derived in part from the German expressionism of the 1920s, imported into the US from Europe by Billy Wilder, Otto Preminger, Robert Siodmak and Fritz Lang. However, a more direct influence in setting and attitudes can be found in the hard-boiled American novels of Dashiell Hammett, Raymond Chandler, James M Cain and Cornell Woolrich.

The films evoked a brutal urban world of crime and corruption in a style that emphasised the depressing locale. The male protagonists, many of them private eyes, are disillusioned loners moving through dimly lit alleyways, rundown hotels, cheerless bars and gaudy nightclubs. All are as corrupt and mercenary as one another. These anti-heroes are tough except when it comes to women – femmes fatales, beautiful and charming but amoral double-dealing dames, who catch them in a web of passion, deceit and murder.

One of the favourite devices is the first-person off-screen narration, especially effective in Billy Wilder's *Double Indemnity* (1944), and taken to its subjective extreme by Robert Montgomery, the director and star of *Lady in the Lake* (1947), the whole story literally seen through Philip Marlowe's eyes. Chandler's detective also appeared in Edward Dmytryk's *Murder My Sweet* (1944), played by Dick Powell, and in Howard Hawks' *The Big Sleep* (1946) he was portrayed by Humphrey Bogart. Bogart was the first star of film noir, having starred as Dashiell Hammett's Sam Spade in John Huston's *The Maltese Falcon* (1941), the film that is considered to have started the whole cycle. In France, the main practitioner was Henri-Georges Clouzot whose films were exceptionally dark in character with a pointed observation of human frailty.

By the early 1950s the classic period had ended but there were still excellent examples of the genre such as Fritz Lang's *The Big Heat* (1953) and *Human Desire* (1954), Robert Aldrich's *Kiss Me Deadly* (1955) and Orson Welles' *Touch of Evil* (1958), all of which had bigger stakes at risk and much nastier characters than in the previous decade; for example, gangster Lee Marvin, in *The Big Heat*, who throws a pot of boiling coffee into his moll Gloria Grahame's face, is one of the most famous scenes in noir history.

Films noir continued to crop up throughout the following decades, often transmuted into other genres such as science fiction in Jean-Luc Godard's

Alphaville (1965) and Ridley Scott's *Blade Runner* (1982). The closest attempt to create a later, pure film noir was Roman Polanski's *Chinatown* (1974). Film noirism was also lampooned, most successfully in Carl Reiner's *Dead Men Don't Wear Plaid* (1982), which cleverly integrated clips from the great period.

KEY WORKS

← **Double Indemnity,** 1944, BILLY WILDER
Insurance man Walter Neff (Fred MacMurray) gets involved with femme fatale Phyllis Dietrichson (Barbara Stanwyck), with whom he plans to kill her husband. They meet surreptitiously each morning at a supermarket. There, they pretend to be shoppers, browsing the shelves while coolly discussing the murder details.

The Maltese Falcon, 1941, JOHN HUSTON [see p.64]
'The stuff that dreams are made of,' says hard-boiled private eye Sam Spade (Humphrey Bogart) when he finally unwraps the treasured objet d'art named the Maltese Falcon, sought after by three shady characters. This brooding, seminal film noir is one of the most assured of directorial debuts and pushed Bogart into the first rank of stars.

OTHER WORKS

Le corbeau (The Raven), 1943, CLOUZOT; **Murder My Sweet,** 1944, DMYTRYK; **Fallen Angel,** 1945, PREMINGER; **The Big Sleep,** 1946, HAWKS; **The Killers,** 1946, SIODMAK; **The Man I Love,** 1946, WALSH; **Lady in the Lake,** 1947, MONTGOMERY; **Out of the Past,** 1947, TOURNEUR; **The Big Heat,** 1953, LANG; **Human Desire,** 1954, LANG; **Kiss Me Deadly,** 1955, ALDRICH; **Touch of Evil,** 1958, WELLES; **Alphaville,** 1965, GODARD; **Chinatown,** 1974, POLANSKI; **Blade Runner,** 1982, RIDLEY SCOTT; **Dead Men Don't Wear Plaid,** 1982, REINER

 Caligarism; Expressionism; Gangsterism; Poetic Realism

 Illusionism; Exoticism; Escapism; Costume Romanticism; Utopianism; Musicalism

🕐 Emotionalist films usually emphasise the emotions of the characters and heighten the dramatic situations of the plot. They focus on crises in everyday life: doomed love affairs, infidelity, unrequited love, family problems or marital separation. These melodramas were often referred to as 'women's pictures' or 'tearjerkers'.

🌑 JOHN STAHL 1886–1950; FRANK BORZAGE 1893–1962; KING VIDOR 1894–1982; DOUGLAS SIRK 1897–1987; EDMUND GOULDING 1891–1959; JOAN CRAWFORD 1904–77; BARBARA STANWYCK 1907–90; BETTE DAVIS 1908–89; MARGARET SULLAVAN 1909–60; RAINER WERNER FASSBINDER 1946–82; PEDRO ALMODÓVAR 1949–

🕐 everyday crises; non-diegetic music; strong female characters; stylised acting

🌑 Emotionalism has a long tradition in cinema from the days of DW Griffith, whose *Way Down East* (1920), with Lillian Gish as an orphan girl turned out in the cold, drew on Victorian stage melodrama. However, it reached levels of sophistication in the 1930s through to the 1950s, peaking with the glossy tearjerkers of Douglas Sirk such as *All That Heaven Allows* (1955).

In between the male-orientated war films and westerns that Hollywood turned out in the 1930s and 1940s, was the 'woman's picture'. Producers thought women would be more interested than men in relationships, love and marriage empathising with the onscreen sufferings of strong female protagonists. The formula allowed the characters, socially victimised or handicapped, to work through their

difficulties and surmount the problems with steadfast bravery. The heroines were often mothers, cruelly neglected and scorned by their children, or separated from them because of financial or social pressures. Much of these depended on the leading lady pulling out all the stops, with Bette Davis, Joan Crawford and Barbara Stanwyck reigning supreme, the latter the victim of the class system in *Stella Dallas* (1937).

Since these emotional Hollywood films appeared during the period of the proscriptive Hays Code, the ethical guidelines issued to the studios from 1930 to 1968, sexual desires and transgressions, children born out of wedlock, rapes and adulteries could only be referred to obliquely. Nevertheless, there was, in the best of them, an implicit condemnation of hypocritical middle-class mores.

Frank Borzage's forte was for bitter-sweet romances with lovers fighting against adversity. His best work came in the 1930s, especially the four movies he made with the delicate, tragic actress Margaret Sullavan. John Stahl, in the same decade, dealt tastefully with novelletish material with the emotions kept at the right pitch, except for his less restrained and more baroque *Leave Her to Heaven* (1945) in which he revelled in Technicolor for the first time. The latter was closer to Douglas Sirk's classic rich and ripe melodramas of the 1950s, three of them remakes of Stahl's versions. These reached the end of Hollywood's golden era of emotionalism.

The German Rainer Werner Fassbinder and the Spanish Pedro Almodóvar later retrospectively embraced the flamboyant style and plot absurdities of the Sirkian soap operas, while Todd Haynes' *Far From Heaven* (2002) was an admiring pastiche.

KEY WORKS

↑ **All That Heaven Allows,** 1955, DOUGLAS SIRK
Jane Wyman, a wealthy widow, is ostracised by her peers and condemned by her adult children when she becomes involved with her gardener (Rock Hudson), a younger man. Sirk's lush soap opera is also a thinly disguised critique of American suburbia and the oppression of middle-class women.

← **Stella Dallas,** 1937, KING VIDOR
Barbara Stanwyck at the heart-breaking climax of the film as the now ageing Stella, who steps out of the way in order not to spoil her daughter's chances of wealth and position. Here, in the rain, she is stopped by a policeman while taking a peek at her daughter's wedding celebrations to which she was not invited.

OTHER WORKS
Way Down East, 1920, GRIFFITH; **Seventh Heaven,** 1927, BORZAGE; **Now Voyager,** 1942, RAPPER; **Dark Victory,** 1939, GOULDING; **Leave Her to Heaven,** 1945, STAHL; **Mildred Pierce,** 1945, CURTIZ ; **Fear Eats the Soul,** 1973, FASSBINDER; **All About My Mother,** 1999, ALMODÓVAR; **Far From Heaven,** 2002, HAYNES

 Hollywood Studioism; Costume Romanticism; Classicism; Eroticism; Escapism

 Avant-Gardism; Horrorism; Realism; Experimentalism; Minimalism

🕐 The biopic (biographical picture) is, on the whole, a rather fanciful narrative of the life of a famous figure. By its very nature, biographism exists in all genres. Yet there are characteristics that mark the biopic out as a genre on its own, such as the narrative technique that places obstacles on the way to eventual success.

◑ **ABEL GANCE** 1889–1981; **WILLIAM DIETERLE** 1893–1972; **PAUL MUNI** 1895–1967; **CHARLES VIDOR** 1900–59; **MIKHAIL ROMM** 1901–77; **RICHARD ATTENBOROUGH** 1923–; **KEN RUSSELL** 1927–; **MILO? FORMAN** 1932–

🕐 content over style; didactic; linear narratives; uplifting

● There are certain narrative principles that govern the conventional biopic. The protagonist risks all for success, endures a period of neglect, then achieves success, usually against all odds. Otherwise, the protagonist falls from the height of fame and makes a triumphant comeback after experiencing personal conflict or becoming afflicted in some way.

A certain amount of veracity is expected of biopics; though events are heightened dramatically, time is telescoped and some characters are amalgams. Biopics hardly ever claim to be 'true to life' as biographical documentaries do. They also differ from films which are 'based on a true story', and which often veer off into a greater fictional dimension. Biopics stick, more or less, to the basic thread of truth while altering many of the facts. They also tend to be inspirational, making audiences draw certain lessons from the lives depicted, or as overt propaganda as in the many Soviet films which featured Lenin: for example, Mikhail Romm's *Lenin in October* (1937) and *Lenin in 1918* (1939) starring Lenin look-alike Boris Shchukin.

In many cases, the actors have to bear some resemblance to the biographical subject or be transformed by make-up. Historical figures such as Napoleon and Lincoln are immediately recognisable whoever plays them, but it is rather more difficult to convince as celebrated actors, pop singers or sports stars whose faces and behaviour are extremely familiar. Kirk Douglas in Vincente Minnelli's *Lust for Life* (1956) needed little make-up to resemble Vincent van Gogh.

Biopics have existed since the earliest days of silent cinema in films such as Georges Méliès' feature-length epic *Jeanne D'Arc* (1899). They cross many genres, such as war films (*Patton*, 1970), musicals (*The Jolson Story*, 1946), westerns (*The True Story of Jesse James*, 1957); costume drama (*Napoleon*, 1927), gangster movies (*Al*

KEY WORKS

← **Lust for Life**, 1956, VINCENTE MINNELLI
Kirk Douglas shows his uncanny physical likeness to Vincent van Gogh. Minnelli magnificently recreates the paintings, despite having lost the battle with MGM to avoid CinemaScope because Van Gogh's paintings were not in the shape that the wide screen demands. However, he managed to substitute Ansco colour for Eastman colour to better capture the artist's works.

→ **Lawrence of Arabia**, 1962, DAVID LEAN
The intelligent and spectacular epic made Peter O'Toole, in the title role, and Omar Sharif (right) international stars overnight. Lean, like his hero, responded to the beauties of the vast Sahara Desert, splendidly caught in all its shifting moods by the camera of Freddy Young.

↙ **The Life of Emile Zola**, 1937, WILLIAM DIETERLE
Paul Muni, who played several great men, is seen as the French writer Émile Zola after a courtroom speech in which he delivers his famous 'J'accuse' exhortation, condemning the military hierarchy for wrongly imprisoning Captain Dreyfus on Devil's Island.

OTHER WORKS
Jeanne D'Arc, 1899, MÉLIÈS; The Story of Louis Pasteur, 1936, DIETERLE; Lenin in October, 1937, ROMM; Napoleon, 1927, GANCE; Juarez, 1939, DIETERLE; Young Mr Lincoln, 1939, FORD; Hudson's Bay, 1941, PICHEL; Yankee Doodle Dandy, 1942, CURTIZ; A Song To Remember, 1945, CHARLES VIDOR; The Jolson Story, 1946, GREEN; The True Story of Jesse James, 1957, NICHOLAS RAY; Al Capone, 1959, WILSON; Patton, 1970, SCHAFFNER; Mahler, 1974, RUSSELL; Gandhi, 1982, ATTENBOROUGH; Amadeus, 1984, FORMAN; The Last Emperor, 1987, BERTOLUCCI; Malcolm X, 1992, SPIKE LEE; The Aviator, 2004, SCORSESE; Ray, 2004, HACKFORD; Milk, 2008, VAN SANT

Capone, 1959), the epic (*Lawrence of Arabia*, 1962), and historical drama (*Young Mr Lincoln*, 1939). In Britain, Ken Russell made a name for himself with his biopics of composers, first on television and then on the large screen.

It was German-born William Dieterle who set the pattern with numerous inspirational biopics of great men. His most successful starred Paul Muni behind heavy make-up in *The Story of Louis Pasteur* (1936), *The Life of Emile Zola* (1937) and *Juarez* (1939). Muni also portrayed French explorer Pierre Radisson in *Hudson's Bay* (1941), and Chopin's music teacher in Charles Vidor's *A Song To Remember* (1945), one of many inaccurate biopics of great composers.

From the 1980s, biopics became more and more popular, and were more concerned with reality than previously. But, as the American critic Roger Ebert wrote: 'Those who seek the truth about a man from the film of his life might as well seek it from his loving grandmother.'

 Documentarism; Hollywood Studioism; Propagandism; Costume Romanticism; Classicism

 Screwballism; Avant-Gardism; Surrealism; Realism; New Wavism

4

THE POST-WAR ERA
1946–59

Neo-realism reacted against the artistic limitations of the Italian film industry during and immediately after the Second World War. The characteristics of neo-realist films were a semi-documentary style, the use of both professional and non-professional actors, real locations and episodic plots depicting the everyday problems of working people.

VITTORIO DE SICA 1902–74; **CESARE ZAVATTINI** 1902–89; **LUCHINO VISCONTI** 1906–76; **ROBERTO ROSSELLINI** (1906–77; SUSO CECCHI D'AMICO 1914–; **GIUSEPPE DE SANTIS** 1917–77; **FEDERICO FELLINI** 1920–93; **PIER PAOLO PASOLINI** 1922–75

location; low budget; natural light; non-actors; social themes

The term 'neo-realism' was first used by Antonio Pietrangeli to apply to Luchino

Visconti's *Ossessione* (1942), a coolly observed melodrama based on James M Cain's novel *The Postman Always Rings Twice* (1934). Visconti came closer to the neo-realist ideal with *La Terra Trema* (1948), with its picture of the wretched economic conditions of Sicilian fishermen enacted by local people.

The movement actually began with Roberto Rossellini's *Rome, Open City* (1945), shot in a semi-documentary style under very difficult conditions during the last days of the German occupation of Italy. Rossellini's film, and those by him and others that followed, were seen as a reaction against the wartime Italian cinema dominated by smooth empty entertainments dubbed 'white telephone films'. Jean Cocteau called neo-realist films 'Arabian Nights tales in which the camera would roam the streets dressed as a beggar'.

Due to the episodic plots, which were meant to convey the rhythm of everyday life, unobtrusive camera and editing techniques, and the naturalness of the settings and the performers, neo-realism had an intensity and immediacy that audiences had never previously experienced. According to Rossellini: 'The subject of the Neo-Realist film is the world; not story or narrative. It contains no preconceived thesis, because ideas are born in the film from the subject. It has no affinity with the superfluous and the merely spectacular, which it refuses, but is attracted to the concrete.'

The first foreign film to win an honorary Academy Award was *Shoeshine* (1946), which dealt with juvenile poverty, which its director, Vittorio De Sica, followed with *Bicycle Thieves* (1948), justifiably the most celebrated of the neo-realist films. Its touching simplicity and underlying social criticism gave it wide appeal. De Sica's *Umberto D* (1952), which traces the struggles and humiliations of an old-age pensioner's struggle to subsist, was the last important neo-realist film of the period.

Screenwriters Cesare Zavattini and Suso Cecchi D'Amico were influences on De Sica and Visconti respectively. Federico Fellini had his roots in neo-realism – he wrote scripts for Rossellini – before creating his own mythology. Giuseppe De Santis, who co-wrote *Ossessione*, contributed *Days of Glory* (1945) and *Bitter Rice* (1949) to the impressive movement. Some younger Italian directors, such as Pier Paolo Pasolini, Ermanno Olmi and Francesco Rosi, continued the tradition in their own individual ways, however the influence of Italian neo-realism on directors from countries as diverse as the UK, India, Brazil and, most recently, Iran, is inestimable.

KEY WORKS

↑ **Bicycle Thieves,** 1948, VITTORIO DE SICA
A long-time unemployed man (Lamberto Maggiorani) is offered a job as a bill-sticker as long as he has a bicycle. Here, with his son (Enzo Staiola), he is off to work with the bicycle bought from a pawnbroker in exchange for the family linen. The film contains one of the most believable and moving portrayals of a father–son relationship in all cinema.

← **Rome, Open City,** 1945, ROBERTO ROSSELLINI
Anna Magnani, one of the few professionals in the cast, is Pina, a pregnant woman who gives refuge to a Resistance leader, and is finally shot by soldiers of the Wehrmacht. An exceptional immediacy and intensity was created by Rossellini, who used a documentary approach, shooting with minimum resources in the streets and apartments of Rome.

OTHER WORKS

Ossessione, 1942, VISCONTI; **Days of Glory,** 1945, DE SANTIS; **Shoeshine,** 1946, DE SICA; **Paisa,** 1947, ROSSELLINI; **La Terra Trema,** 1948, VISCONTI; **Bitter Rice,** 1949, DE SANTIS; **Umberto D,** 1952, DE SICA; **La Strada,** 1954, FELLINI; **Accatone,** 1961, PASOLINI

 Poetic Realism; Naturalism; Realism; New Wavism; Dogmetism

 Illusionism; Monumentalism; Expressionism; Hollywood Studioism; Costume Romanticism

Hollywood, once known as the Dream Factory, attempted to interpret the phrase 'Life, liberty, and the pursuit of happiness' as enshrined in the American Constitution. Utopian films demonstrated the notion of a perfect society that survives all attempts at despoliation and culminates in the obligatory 'happy ending'.

CECIL B DEMILLE 1881–1959; **HENRY KING** 1888–1982; **JOHN FORD** 1894–1973; **FRANK CAPRA** 1897–1991; **EMERIC PRESSBURGER** 1902–88; **VINCENTE MINNELLI** 1903–86; **MICHAEL POWELL** 1905–90; **SERGEI PARAJANOV** 1924–90

conservative values; optimism; patriotism; small town versus big city

Utopian films present an integrated, stable community, composed of individuals who make sacrifices for one another and for the town as a whole. However, the order and stability of a Utopia must be fought for against outside forces. This is demonstrated by Cecil B DeMille's westerns between 1937 and 1947 – energetic, unsubtle patriotic celebrations of the frontiersmen of America carving out a paradise – and John Ford and Henry King's nostalgic evocations of rural and small-town America such as *Steamboat Round the Bend* (1935) and *State Fair* (1933) respectively. Characters create utopian spaces, fighting off anyone who tries to invade them. American virtue is often represented by small towns where Christian values are held up as the ideal. Hollywood's utopian vision of small-town life – showing white picket fences in front of homes of honest, loving families who attend the local church and school – is often threatened by the evils of the big city.

Frank Capra's populist films like *Mr Deeds Goes to Town* (1936) and *Mr Smith Goes to Washington* (1939) draw sharp contrasts between the values of the small town and the big city, where corruption and greed prevail. The logical extension of Capra's social views is *Lost Horizon* (1937), set in an actual Utopia, or Shangri-La, which lies in a gorgeous valley where the sun always shines and where the contented people have found spiritual enlightenment.

Capra's *It's A Wonderful Life* (1946)

shows what happens when Bedford Falls becomes Pottersville, the town's dark alternative. The diurnal iconography of small-town America is replaced by the nocturnal one of film noir with police sirens, strip clubs and sordid bars. The happy family in Santa Rosa in Alfred Hitchcock's *Shadow of a Doubt* (1943) is invaded by Uncle

KEY WORKS

↑ **It's A Wonderful Life,** 1946, FRANK CAPRA
At the sentimental ending – all tearful smiles and pealing bells – 'the little man' George Bailey (James Stewart, centre) celebrates with his wife (Donna Reed), children and neighbours, his return to Bedford Falls from a hypothetical time to the present, when he finds that the people of the town have collected enough money to pay off his debts.

Charlie's big-city ways. In both films, George Bailey (James Stewart) and Young Charlie (Teresa Wright), respectively, suffer because they cannot see the utopian aspects of their towns and wish to be elsewhere.

In contrast, in Vincente Minnelli's *Meet Me in St Louis* (1944) the children and wife of a businessman are distraught when he announces that he is getting a job in New York. Finally, the paterfamilias realises that everything they want is in St Louis. At the World's Fair, Esther (Judy Garland) says: 'I can't believe it. Right here where we live. Right here in St Louis,' echoing Garland's Dorothy, who says: 'There is no place like home' at the end of *The Wizard of Oz* (1939). Minnelli's *Yolanda and the Thief* (1945) and *Brigadoon* (1954) each take

place in Utopias, the former a Latin American wonderland called Patria, the latter an enchanted Scottish village that emerges once a century from the mists.

The musical offered audiences the idea of a Utopia where the negative aspects of the real world, such as poverty, prejudice and crime, are nonexistent. They created a never-never land free from the restrictions that govern our normal daily lives.

In Britain, Michael Powell and Emeric Pressburger's films: *The Life and Death of Colonel Blimp* (1943), *A Canterbury Tale* (1944), *I Know Where I'm Going* (1945) and *A Matter of Life and Death* (1946) revealed an almost mystical love of the nation, which goes against the British realist tradition. Utopianism is also connected to many of the

↑ **Meet Me in St Louis,** 1944, VINCENTE MINNELLI
Judy Garland (centre), then Minnelli's wife, sings the rhythmically staged 'The Trolly Song' watched admiringly by 'boy next door' Tom Drake. Using Technicolor for the first time, Minnelli was able to paint the four seasons in the year of a St Louis family between 1902 and 1903 with a loving eye for period detail.

idealised societies created under dictatorships such as Nazi Germany and the Soviet Union. The film that perhaps best illustrates this is Yakov Protazanov's *Aelita* (1924), in which two Russian soldiers land on Mars and organise a revolution on the Soviet model, optimistically viewing the future from the standpoint of the USSR's New Economic Policy.

Far from the Soviet model, the Georgian director Sergei Parajanov explored the history and folklore of his native land through lyrical and opulent imagery. As a friend of his remarked: 'Parajanov made films not about how things are, but how they would have been had he been God.'

State Fair, 1933, HENRY KING
Lew Ayres and Janet Gaynor fall in love on the rollercoaster in one of Henry King's finest examples of Americana, extolling community life, honesty, humour and hard work. It was remade as an equally wholesome Technicolor musical in 1945.

OTHER WORKS
Aelita, 1924, PROTAZANOV; Steamboat Round the Bend, 1935, FORD; Mr Deeds Goes to Town, 1936, CAPRA; Lost Horizon, 1937, CAPRA; Mr Smith Goes to Washington, 1939, CAPRA; The Wizard of Oz, 1939, FLEMING; The Life and Death of Colonel Blimp, 1943, POWELL/PRESSBURGER; Shadow of a Doubt, 1943, HITCHCOCK; A Canturbury Tale, 1944, POWELL/PRESSBURGER; I Know Where I'm Going, 1945, POWELL/PRESSBURGER; Yolanda and the Thief, 1945, MINNELLI; A Matter of Life and Death, 1946, POWELL/PRESSBURGER; Brigadoon, 1954, MINNELLI; The Colour of Pomegranates, 1969, PARAJANOV

 Hollywood Studioism; Escapism; Musicalism; Costume Romanticism; Socialist Realism

 Expressionism; Horrorism; Gangsterism; Film Noirism; Dystopianism

The western, the oldest of all film genres, has shown remarkable adaptability to changing times. The strength of westernism lay in its continuity, the familiarity of the material and its imagery. Despite variations in ideas and style, westerns are united by the accepted conventions.

RAOUL WALSH 1887–80; JOHN FORD 1894–1973; HOWARD HAWKS 1896–1977; RANDOLPH SCOTT 1898–1987; ANTHONY MANN 1906–67; JOHN WAYNE 1907–79; JOHN STURGES 1910–92; BUDD BOETTICHER 1916–2001; SAM PECKINPAH 1925–84; SERGIO LEONE 1929–89; CLINT EASTWOOD 1930–

good versus evil; location shooting; man versus nature; solitary heroes

The geographical location of westerns is usually west of the Mississippi River, north of the Rio Grande and south of the border with Mexico. The historical setting is traditionally the 1850s to the 1890s, a period that saw the Dakota and Californian gold rushes, the American Civil War, the building of the Transcontinental Railroad, the Indian wars, the opening up of the cattle ranges, the range wars and the steady spread westwards of homesteaders, farmers and immigrants. It also saw the virtual extermination of the buffalo and most of the indigenous Native American tribes. However, some westerns extend back to the time of America's colonial era or forward to the mid-20th century.

To many Americans it was their country's most exciting time. The most fundamental theme of the western is the civilising of the wilderness and its occupants. In other words, it told how the West was won.

Westerns narrate the exploits, on both sides of the law, of Wyatt Earp, Doc Holliday, Wild Bill Hickock, Calamity Jane, Bat Masterson, the James Brothers (Frank and Jesse) and Billy the Kid, all of whom existed. But, as the newspaperman says in John Ford's *The Man Who Shot Liberty Valance* (1962): 'When the legend becomes fact, print the legend.' From the time of the first narrative screen western, Edward S Porter's *The Great Train Robbery* (1903), the legends of the West had already become embedded in American popular culture.

Among the iconic elements are remote forts and vast ranches, and the small town, with its one hotel, one saloon, one attractive unmarried woman, one moral man, one jail and the main street where the inevitable showdown between hero and villain takes place. However, many of the best westerns have a psychological complexity that stretches beyond the simplistic 'good versus evil' premise towards the dimensions of Greek tragedy.

The golden age of the western began with John Ford's *Stagecoach* (1939) and ended with his *The Searchers* (1956), both appropriately starring John Wayne, the actor most associated with Ford and with the genre. Howard Hawks also expropriated Wayne for several more contained films, including *Rio Bravo* (1959). The great period included five films by Anthony Mann, starring a new, tougher, more bitter James Stewart, and Budd Boetticher's seven taut westerns with Randolph Scott.

In the 1960s, America was a nation in flux. The war in Vietnam altered the perspective on frontier heroics, the Indian wars and the morality play between good and evil. In a more cynical age, America's

confidence in its past, on which westernism depended, began to ebb. The genre was kept alive by Sam Peckinpah's nostalgic but harsh views of the Old West, the so-called 'spaghetti westerns', which brought Clint Eastwood stardom. Eastwood's *Unforgiven* (1992) is thought to be the last word on the western.

KEY WORKS

← **Stagecoach,** 1939, JOHN FORD
This western raised the genre to artistic status with its characterisation of nine people travelling through dangerous Indian territory. In this beautifully composed studio shot, George Bancroft (left) is the sheriff having to arrest the Ringo Kid (John Wayne), held by doomed hooker Dallas (Claire Trevor, right).

↙ **Unforgiven,** 1992, CLINT EASTWOOD
Clint Eastwood as a poor widower with two small children, trying to scratch a living off the land. The movie is Eastwood's repudiation of his violent persona, and a deglamorisation of the West, seeing it as a dirty, brutal place.

OTHER WORKS
The Great Train Robbery, 1903, PORTER; My Darling Clementine, 1946, FORD; Red River, 1948, HAWKS; Colorado Territory, 1949, WALSH; She Wore a Yellow Ribbon, 1949, FORD; The Gunfighter, 1950, KING; High Noon, 1952, ZINNEMANN; Shane, 1953, STEVENS; The Man From Laramie, 1955, MANN; The Searchers, 1956, FORD; The Big Country, 1958, WYLER; Ride Lonesome, 1959, BOETTICHER; Rio Bravo, 1959, HAWKS; The Magnificent Seven, 1960, JOHN STURGES; The Man Who Shot Liberty Valance, 1962, FORD; Once Upon a Time in the West, 1968, LEONE; The Wild Bunch, 1969, PECKINPAH; Little Big Man, 1970, PENN; Dances with Wolves, 1990, COSTNER

 Athleticism; Hollywood Studioism; Costume Romanticism; Racialism; Classicism

 Avant-Gardism; Surrealism; Film Noirism; Experimentalism; Minimalism

Born with the coming of sound, the Hollywood movie musical derived from two sources: opera and operetta, brought over by European émigrés, and the American tradition of vaudeville, the inspiration behind so many 'backstage' musicals, the plots of which revolved around putting on a show.

ERNST LUBITSCH 1892–1947; ARTHUR FREED 1894–1973; BUSBY BERKELEY 1895–1976; RENÉ CLAIR 1898–1981; GRIGORI ALEXANDROV 1903–83; VINCENTE MINNELLI 1910–86; CHARLES WALTERS 1911–82; GENE KELLY 1912–96; GEORGE SIDNEY 1916–2002; STANLEY DONEN 1924–; BOB FOSSE 1927–87); JACQUES DEMY 1931–90

avoidance of realism; diegetic music; lavish staging; lightweight plots

The curious alliance between dream and reality in the musical gave directors, designers and cinematographers the most creative scope within the commercial structure of Hollywood. They were able to experiment with chiaroscuro, colour, trompe l'oeil, split-screen techniques, superimposition, trick photography, surreal settings and animation. This made the musical an important force in imaginative filmmaking, without it being accused of 'avant-gardism' by cautious studio moguls.

Musicals could also easily circumvent the censorious Hays Code, instigated in 1930 as a moral guideline for the studios. The code proclaimed: 'Dances which suggest or represent sexual actions, whether

performed solo or with two or more; dances intended to excite the emotional reaction of the audience … violate decency and are wrong.' 'Costumes intended to permit undue exposure' were also condemned. But the history of the film musical is full of such 'shocking' dances. Scantily dressed women and sexual innuendo almost went unnoticed by the censors as long as they remained within the seemingly harmless confines of the musical as if nothing indecorous could happen in the context of the make-believe world the family entertainment inhabited.

It was the studio system that enabled these sumptuous dreams to take shape. Paramount, the most European of the studios in the 1930s, encouraged Ernst Lubitsch to bring his continental manners and hedonism to bear on the musical, culminating in *The Merry Widow* (1934). RKO highlighted the Fred Astaire-Ginger Rogers dancing duo in nine black-and-white musicals between 1933 and 1939. Set

KEY WORKS

↑ **On the Town,** 1949, STANLEY DONEN, GENE KELLY
The opening sequence, filmed on location, something unheard of in those days, in which (from left to right) Gene Kelly, Frank Sinatra and Jules Munshin arrive for 24 hours' leave in New York. It seemed perfectly logical, in terms of the integrated musical, that they should manifest their joy by literally singing the praises of that 'wonderful town'.

← **The Merry Widow,** 1934, ERNST LUBITSCH
At Maxim's in Paris, the famous cafe synonymous with the gaiety and glamour of the city, enhanced by the 'Lubitsch Touch', Maurice Chevalier as Count Danilo, in the arms of a showgirl (Minna Gombell), gets a searing look from Jeannette MacDonald in the title role as the wealthy widow Sonia pretending to be a resident beauty named Fifi.

against polished art-deco sets, each of their duets were mini-dramas containing all the attraction, antagonism and romance of a relationship – symbolic representations of love-making.

Warner Bros was more economical, fast-paced and down to earth, contrasting the lives of hard-working chorus girls living in cheap apartments with the lavish productions of the shows, choreographed by Busby Berkeley, in which they appeared. Berkeley created the musical numbers purely in terms of the one mobile camera, dollying in erotically on the lines of identically dressed girls, and forming kaleidoscopic effects with high overhead shots from a mobile crane.

What distinguished the films that burst forth from MGM in the 1940s and 1950s, mostly under the producer Arthur Freed, was the integration of musical numbers into the film's narrative. In these features – the best being directed by Charles Walters, George Sidney, Vincente Minnelli, Stanley Donen and Gene Kelly – song, dance and music no longer punctuated the plot but actually worked to advance it. Minnelli triumphed with *An American in Paris* (1951) and the Donen-Kelly partnership produced *On the Town* (1949), the opening number of which was filmed on location in New York.

At the end of the 1960s, the musical, like the western, became a rare phenomenon, though there was a limited revival of the genre in the 1970s with *Saturday Night Fever* (1977) and *Grease* (1978), and former dancer and choreographer Bob Fosse's *Cabaret* (1972) and *All That Jazz* (1979).

The Hollywood musical had some influence in Europe and vice versa: in Germany (its biggest stars being Swedish-born Zarah Leander and British-born Lilian Harvey) and the Soviet Union, Grigori Alexandrov was a Stalin favourite with four Hollywood-style musicals. In France, Jacques Demy took his inspiration directly from it. However, *The Umbrellas of Cherbourg* (1964), in which all the dialogue was sung, was intrinsically French. On the other hand, René Clair's musical comedies of the early 1930s influenced the development of the Hollywood musical with their use of related action and songs.

← **An American in Paris** 1951, VINCENTE MINNELLI
French ballet dancer Leslie Caron was discovered by Gene Kelly, who got her to partner him in a duet and in the ambitious final 18-minute ballet. Here her classical training immediately makes an impact in her introductory dance solo.

OTHER WORKS
Le million, 1931, CLAIR; Love me Tonight, 1932, MAMOULIAN; 42nd Street, 1933, BACON; Jazz Comedy, 1934, ALEXANDROV; Singin' in the Rain, 1952, DONEN/KELLY; West Side Story, 1961, WISE/ROBBINS; The Umbrellas of Cherbourg, 1964, DEMY; Cabaret, 1972, FOSSE; Saturday Night Fever, 1977, BADHAM; Grease, 1978, KLEISER; All That Jazz, 1979, FOSSE; Moulin Rouge, 2001, LUHRMANN

 Illusionism; Athleticism; Hollywood Studioism; Escapism; Utopianism

 Naturalism; Realism; Film Noirism; Dystopianism; Minimalism

Although the Far East, particularly Japan, had been making films of high quality since the beginnings of cinema, they remained virtually unknown in the West until the 1950s. Since then there has been a growing tide of films from the East that have influenced occidental cinema and vice versa.

KENJI MIZOGUCHI 1898–1956; YASUJIRO OZU 1903–63; AKIRA KUROSAWA 1912–98; SHOHEI IMAMURA 1926–2006; NAGISA ÔSHIMA 1932–; IM KWON-TAEK 1936–; JOHN WOO 1946–; ZHANG YIMOU 1951–; KAIGE CHEN 1952–; ANG LEE 1954–; WONG KAR-WAI 1958–; KIM KI-DUK 1960–; CHAN-WOOK PARK 1963–

period dramas; sexual permissiveness; tradition; violence

Of all the countries in the Far East, Japan has been the most prominent and influential producer of both commercial and artistic films worldwide. Until the 1980s, China produced relatively few internationally known films, whereas its neighbours, Hong Kong and Taiwan, had become renowned for their martial arts movies some two decades previously. South Korean cinema only established its distinctive character in the mid-1990s with the films of Im Kwon-Taek, Kim Ki-Duk and Chan-Wook Park. Now oriental films, regardless of their geographical provenance, loom large in the world cinema landscape. It also could be claimed that the epicentre of cinema shifted from West to East in the 21st century.

Orientalism

Foreign audiences were largely unaware of Japanese films until the breakthrough came when Akira Kurosawa's *Rashomon* (1950) won the Grand Prix at Venice. The intriguing drama, which demonstrated the subjective nature of truth, opened up the floodgate of Japanese films to the West. Kurosawa became the best-known Japanese director in the West possibly because of his greater proximity to occidental culture than that of his compatriots. Three of his films have been transferred easily into westerns: two as spaghetti westerns and one as *The Magnificent Seven* (1960) from *The Seven Samurai* (1954). Some of his own films were homages to American movies and pulp fiction, as well as his two transmutations of Shakespeare plays set in medieval Japan.

For a long time the contrasting Kurosawa, Kenji Mizoguchi and Yasujiro Ozu reined supreme among Japanese directors. For most of its history, Japanese cinema was divided into two categories: *gendai-geki* (films in a contemporary setting) and *jidai-geki* (period films usually set in the Tokugawa era from 1616 to 1868, before the opening of Japan to Western influence). Kurosawa straddled both genres, Mizoguchi expressed his humanist view of feudal Japan mainly through the suffering of women, and Ozu remained a gentle observer of the modern middle-class family.

Parallel to the French New Wave were younger directors such as Nagisa Ôshima and Shohei Imamura, both of whom extended the sexual revolution beyond that in the West. The use of violence also went further than in Western films; aside from the popular 'chop socky' martial arts movies from Taiwan and Hong Kong, though, there was to be more and more cross-fertilisation between the cultures. Directors like the Taiwanese Ang Lee, the Chinese Wong Kar-Wai and John Woo from Hong Kong move

easily between East and West.

China emerged from the Cultural Revolution to become a cinematic force to be reckoned with. The best directors belonged to what was called the Fifth Generation, those who graduated from the Beijing Film Academy in the late 1970s such as Zhang Yimou and Kaige Chen. At the turn of the 21st century, Far Eastern films continued to win prizes at festivals and to attract large audiences.

KEY WORKS

Rashomon, 1950, AKIRA KUROSAWA [see p.84]
Toshiro Mifune as the bandit prepares to rape Machiko Kyo before killing her samurai husband. At the murder trial, the incident is described in four conflicting yet equally credible versions. The title *Rashomon* has come to stand for any story told from different viewpoints.

← **Tokyo Story,** 1953, YASUJIRO OZU
Chishu Ryu (left) and Chieko Higashiyama (right), an elderly couple from south Japan, paying a visit to their children and grandchildren in Tokyo, are not shown much affection except by their widowed daughter-in-law Setsuko Hara (centre). Shot with as little camera movement as possible, and at floor level, with minimum exteriors, it is a moving and perceptive investigation into the tensions within a family and old age.

OTHER WORKS

The Life of Oharu, 1952, MIZOGUCHI; **Ugetsu Monogatari,** 1953, MIZOGUCHI; **The Seven Samurai,** 1954, KUROSAWA; **An Autumn Afternoon,** 1962, OZU; **Raise the Red Lantern,** 1991, YIMOU; **Farewell My Concubine,** 1993, CHEN; **Chungking Express,** 1994, KAR-WAI; **Eat Drink Man Woman,** 1994, ANG LEE; **In the Mood for Love,** 2000, KAR-WAI; **Chihwaseon,** 2002, KWON-TAEK; **Spring, Summer, Autumn, Winter … and Spring,** 2003, KI-DUK

 Athleticism; Exoticism; Emotionalism; Costume Romanticism; Asian Minimalism

 Constructivism; Hollywood Studioism; Westernism; Musicalism; American Indieism

Experimentalism can be distinguished principally by the absence of narrative, the use of techniques such as out of focus, painting or scratching on film, jump cuts and asynchronous sound, and little interest in an audience.

MAYA DEREN 1917–61; **JONAS MEKAS** 1922–; **GREGORY MARKOPOULOS** 1928–92; **ANDY WARHOL** 1928–87; **MICHAEL SNOW** 1929–; **STAN BRAKHAGE** 1933–2003; **BRUCE CONNER** 1933–2008; **HOLLIS FRAMPTON** 1936–84; **GEORGE KUCHAR** 1942–; **JON JOST** 1943–

minimal budget; non-narrative; rhythmic editing; subjectivity

Experimentalism is anathema to popular and mainstream culture. Most experimental films give primacy to the visual, using sound in non-naturalistic ways. Many experimental directors prefer to think of films as metaphorical, abstract and highly subjective – a kind of poetry written with light. Their aim is to redefine our way of seeing by exploring new spatio-temporal concepts. The films are made on very low budgets, with a minimal crew, and the filmmaker generally edits and distributes the film him- or herself. The abstract films of the

European avant-garde in the 1920s inspired later experimentalism in France and the US.

In France, Isidore Isou, founder of the Lettrists, whose *Venom and Eternity* caused riots at the 1951 Cannes Film Festival, stated: 'I announce the destruction of the cinema.' His film consisted of four and a half hours of 'discordant' images, enhanced with scratches, shaky footage, blank frames, stock shots and a soundtrack consisting of monologues and onomatopoeic poetry.

Meshes of the Afternoon (1943) by Maya Deren and Alexander Hammid is considered to be one of the first important American experimental films. It consists of four disjunctive trance-like sequences as a woman (Deren) steps from beach to grass to mud to pavement to rug. Deren believed that cinema is the art of the 'controlled accident', the 'delicate balance between spontaneity and deliberate design in art'. Structural filmmakers Hollis Frampton and Michael Snow created a highly formalist cinema that foregrounded the medium itself: the frame, projection and time breaking film down into bare components. Snow's *Wavelength* (1966) is effectively a single 45-minute zoom starting from a high viewing position, finally focusing on a photograph of the sea. Frampton's largely silent *Zoms Lemma* (1970) shows the viewer an evolving 24-part alphabet composed initially of New York City street signs.

Stan Brakhage's *Dog Star Man* (1964) experimented with the use of colour, painting on film and distorting lenses. For Brakhage, the goal of cinema was the liberation of the eye itself, undefined by conventions of representation. 'Imagine an eye unruled by man-made laws of perspective,' Brakhage wrote in 1963, 'an eye unprejudiced by compositional logic, an eye which does not respond to the name of everything but which must know each

object encountered in life through an adventure of perception'. Inspired mainly by the example of Brakhage, Jonas Mekas created an ongoing cinematic diary, *Diaries, Notes and Sketches.* Jon Jost perfected the film essay, while Bruce Conner experimented with found footage.

Experimentalism can be illustrated at its extremes by Andy Warhol's black-and-white and silent 'anti-films', for example *Sleep* (1963), a study of the poet John Giorno asleep for around six hours, or *Empire* (1964), which shows the Empire State Building from a fixed position for eight hours. The films are projected not at the standard sound speed of 24 frames per second, but at silent speed – 16 frames per second – thus further retarding the minimal action.

Warhol's movies also explored homoerotic themes, as did those of Gregory Markopoulos, George Kuchar and Kenneth Anger, whose gay biker movie *Scorpio Rising* (1964) influenced a swathe of 'queer' underground movies.

KEY WORKS

↑ **Scorpio Rising,** 1964, KENNETH ANGER
One of the leather 'bike-boys' who takes part in an orgy which is juxtaposed with clips from Hollywood films, Nazi symbolism, occultism, and 13 rock songs on the soundtrack. As an example of experimentalism entering the mainstream, Anger's use of jump cuts and pop music was a huge influence on later music videos and commercials.

← **Meshes of the Afternoon,** 1943, MAYA DEREN, ALEXANDER HAMMID
The Ukranian-born Maya Deren in her own film, a study of feminine angst dealing with a suicide which rejects a traditional narrative structure in favour of the logic of a dream. The film, shot with a 16-millimetre Bolex camera, was one of the first of the experimental films that were labelled 'psychodramas'.

OTHER WORKS
Venom and Eternity, 1951, ISOU; **A Movie,** 1958, CONNER; **Sleep,** 1963, WARHOL; **Empire,** 1964, WARHOL; **Dog Star Man,** 1964, BRAKHAGE; **Wavelength,** 1966, SNOW; **Zoms Lemma,** 1970, FRAMPTON

 Avant-Gardism; Surrealism; Auteurism; American Indieism; Minimalism

 Monumentalism; Hollywood Studioism; Escapism; Classicism; Postmodernism

Liberalism

Liberalism in Hollywood began to flower in the 1950s with the coming of more independent producers. The spirit of liberalism was kept alive by some directors in repressive regimes via symbolism and oblique allusions.

ELIA KAZAN 1909–2003; STANLEY KRAMER 1913–2001; MARTIN RITT 1914–90; SIDNEY LUMET 1924–; ANDRZEJ WAJDA 1926–; CARLOS SAURA 1932–; COSTA-GAVRAS 1933–; THEO ANGELOPOULOS 1935–; OLIVER STONE 1946–; MICHAEL MOORE 1954–

anti-establishment; content over style; issue related; optimism

Liberalism in the movies is not a notion that has much meaning outside the US because liberal-themed films are generally defined by their contrast to the conservatism of establishment Hollywood. In the 1950s, when independent producers began to break the stranglehold of the major studios, they were able to tackle more daring subjects and delve into those areas from which Hollywood had previously shied. But it took America a little longer to emerge from the sinister shadow that was cast over the film industry by Joseph McCarthy. As a result of the House Un-American Activities Committee's series of hearings, hundreds of people in Hollywood were blacklisted for their 'communist' affiliations. This took place in the climate of the Cold War, while the hot war in Korea demanded unconditional patriotism from US citizens.

Although Hollywood grew jittery, liberal themes were explored and the tenets on which American society was based were questioned. For example, racial intolerance was examined. Some commercial liberal films were considered very daring, though the critic James Agee called them 'a profitable form of safe fearlessness'. John Ford, not known for his liberal views, made *The Grapes of Wrath* (1940), one of the few films until then that had a social conscience.

It was only after the Second World War that the major studios began to address topics such as poverty, racism and anti-Semitism. In 1949, independent producer Stanley Kramer took on the subject of racism in the US army with *Home of the Brave*, one of the first pictures to do so. Kramer later directed *The Defiant Ones* (1958) and *Guess Who's Coming to Dinner?* (1967), both of which featured Sidney Poitier, the first black star to break away from the negro caricature. Poitier also made an impression as a detective in Norman Jewison's *In The Heat of the Night* (1967), an exposé of racial bigotry in the Deep South.

Martin Ritt, who studied with Elia Kazan, Sidney Lumet from television, and former photographer Stanley Kubrick voiced strong liberal views in Hollywood in the late 1950s. In the late 1960s and early 1970s, during the Vietnam War, several American directors emerged to express more egalitarian notions, while Greek-born Costa-Gavras exposed dictatorial regimes in Greece, Czechoslovakia and South America.

The western was appropriated by directors in order to express their liberal views: Red Indians were seen as representing the Vietcong, and 19th-century negro slaves spoke like members of the Black Power movement. Oliver Stone, combative in almost everything he touches, continued the liberal tradition by attacking *Wall Street* (1987) and American foreign policy, and Michael Moore trod a similar path with his personal documentaries. Andrzej Wajda, Carlos Saura and Theo Angelopoulos managed to make films covertly critical of the Polish Communist regime, Franco's Spain and Greece under the generals.

KEY WORKS

↑ **In the Heat of the Night,** 1967, NORMAN JEWISON
Philadelphia-based police detective Virgil Tibbs (Sidney Poitier, left) finds himself helping Bill Gillespie (Rod Steiger), the redneck police chief of a small Mississippi town in an investigation into the murder of a wealthy white man. A game of dominance is played by the white bigot and the black homicide expert, from which the latter emerges victorious, forcing the former to reconsider his prejudices.

← **The Grapes of Wrath,** 1940, JOHN FORD
Henry Fonda as Tom Joad with Jane Darwell (centre) as his mother and Dorris Bowdon, his sister, in their old jalopy, forced to leave their land in the dustbowl of Oklahoma, heading for the 'promised land' of California. Despite the hardships, in the end Ma Joad says: 'They can't wipe us out. They can't lick us. And we'll go on forever … 'cause … we're the people.'

OTHER WORKS
Gentleman's Agreement, 1947, KAZAN; **Crossfire,** 1949, DYMTRYK; **Home of the Brave,** 1949, KRAMER; **Pinky,** 1949, KAZAN; **Twelve Angry Men,** 1957, LUMET; **The Defiant Ones,** 1958, KRAMER; **To Kill a Mockingbird,** 1963, MULLIGAN; **Dr Strangelove,** 1963, KUBRICK; **Guess Who's Coming to Dinner?,** 1967, KRAMER; **Norma Rae,** 1979, RITT; **Missing,** 1982, COSTA-GAVRAS; **Wall Street,** 1987, STONE; **Born on the Fourth of July,** 1989, STONE; **Sicko,** 2007, MOORE

Realism; Italian Neo-Realism; Anti-Militarism; Utopianism; Feminism

Constructivism; Socialist Realism; Propagandism; Racialism; Postmodernism

The classical style was developed in Hollywood at the start of the golden age of studio production, when certain rules of editing, lighting and narrative were laid down.

ERNST LUBITSCH 1892–1947; JOHN FORD 1894–1973; HOWARD HAWKS 1896–1977; DOUGLAS SIRK 1897–1987; MICHAEL CURTIZ 1888–1962; GEORGE CUKOR 1899–1983; CLAUDE AUTANT-LARA 1901–2000; WILLIAM WYLER 1902–81; VINCENTE MINNELLI 1903–86; OTTO PREMINGER 1905–86; BILLY WILDER 1906–2002; DAVID LEAN 1908–91; JOSEPH L MANKIEWICZ 1909–93; MARCEL CARNÉ 1906–96; MARTIN SCORSESE 1942–

establishing shots; 'invisible' editing; linear narratives; objectivity

Classical cinema is built on representational codes of realism. Unlike more advanced cinema, the style does not draw attention to itself. Editing is intended to be 'invisible' so that the audience is almost unaware of the flow of shots and the manipulation of time and space. The classical style insists on temporal and spatial continuity as a way of advancing narrative, to which every aspect of the film is subordinated. The only permissible manipulation of time is the flashback, mostly used as part of character development, or as the subjective memory of the character. Each sequence classically begins with an establishing shot, moves in to a medium shot and then, if there are two people in the frame, to shot reverse shot and close-ups.

Important characters are seen in the centre of the picture frame and are never out of focus, while other characters create a visual balance. The narrative usually moves on two levels: the relationship, most likely romantic, between characters, and the wider action in which they find themselves. The protagonists progress through psychological motivation to overcome obstacles and reach the obligatory happy ending.

These rules of classicism in the cinema were established in the Hollywood studio system to provide a template to help speed up production and make the films easier to market. Mavericks like Orson Welles, who broke the rules, were not tolerated. Despite the studio restrictions, there were some directors, like John Ford, Howard Hawks, Otto Preminger and Douglas Sirk, whose personalities were strong enough to put their signature on a film, something that led to the formulation of the so-called *auteur* theory by François Truffaut. Others, such as William Wyler, George Cukor and Vincente Minnelli submerged their individuality in order to shape quality classicist films

keeping within the studio style. Michael Curtiz's *Casablanca* (1943) is a prime example. Joseph L Mankiewicz delighted in witty, literate dialogue within the classical model as in *All About Eve* (1950), and Billy Wilder, in the tradition of his mentor Ernst Lubitsch, put a great deal of emphasis on the art of screenwriting and the structuring of plots.

Film classicism still dominates commercial narrative cinema worldwide, ranging from crass commercialism to academic screenplays (for example, those of Ron Howard) to the more adventurous classically made movies of Martin Scorsese, Steven Spielberg and Oliver Stone.

KEY WORKS

← **All About Eve,** 1950, JOSEPH L MANKIEWICZ
From left: Anne Baxter (ambitious Eve Harrington), Bette Davis (ageing stage-star Margo Channing), Marilyn Monroe (aspiring starlet) and George Sanders (the well-named acid theatre critic Addison DeWitt) in a typically witty encounter. They are framed in a classical four-shot because each is as important as the other in the scene.

← **Casablanca,** 1943, MICHAEL CURTIZ
Ilsa (Ingrid Bergman) and Rick (Humphrey Bogart) rekindle their love for one another as she makes one last effort to get the transit papers for her resistance-fighter husband (Paul Henreid) to escape Casablanca. The strong plot, exotic setting, the piquant dialogue and the performances made this one of Warner Bros' greatest hits, which looks even better as time goes by.

OTHER WORKS
Gone with the Wind, 1939, FLEMING; **The Little Foxes,** 1941, WYLER; **Laura,** 1944, PREMINGER; **Les enfants du paradis,** 1945, CARNÉ; **Le diable au corps,** 1947, AUTANT-LARA; **Letter from an Unknown Woman,** 1948, OPHÜLS; **The Bad and the Beautiful,** 1952, MINNELLI; **On the Waterfront,** 1954, KAZAN; **The Apartment,** 1960, WILDER; **Dr Zhivago,** 1966, LEAN; **Taxi Driver,** 1976, SCORSESE

 Hollywood Studioism; Escapism Costume Romanticism; Emotionalism; Biographism

 Expressionism; Avant-Gardism; Surrealism; Experimentalism; Minimalism

Teenagism

Teen pics cover subjects such as the coming of age, first love and conflicts with parents, usually treating these in a glossy manner.

WILLIAM ASHER 1921–; **ROGER CORMAN** 1926–; **RICHARD LESTER** 1932–; **JOHN HUGHES** 1950–2009; **JOHN LANDIS** 1950–

adolescence; alienation; conflict; music; rites of passage; sex

Movies purposefully made to attract teenagers reached their peak in the 1980s, but it was in the 1950s, when American adolescents had more money at their disposal, that producers first recognised that there was a market for youth-orientated films. This tends to be mainly an American film phenomenon, with other countries making many films about teenagers rather than specifically for them. Japanese cinema, in particular, has explored the competitive education system and disaffected youth, through violence, such as Kinji Fukasaku's *Battle Royale* (2001), in which teenage schoolchildren are put on an isolated island and forced to kill each other to survive.

As censorship gradually weakened into the 1960s, subjects like sex could be treated more frankly. Teenagers were typically patronised and ridiculed in films made before the 1950s..

Although pre-1950s films showed teenagers trying to attract the opposite sex and attempting to escape adult control, any meaningful rebellion was non-existent and they would conform in the end.

Youth culture began to infiltrate the movies in the 1950s. It was the era of the rebel, personified by Marlon Brando and James Dean, with whom it was possible for young people to identify for the first time. Dean resonated most. It was also the period of the juvenile delinquent, where teenagers were seen in terms of social problems. This was allied to rock 'n' roll which burst onto the screen in Richard Brooks' *Blackboard Jungle* (1955).

In the next decade there came a series of beach-party movies, most of them directed by William Asher, in which the plots usually involved a group of young, scantily clad surfers defending their right to continue their love-ins and gyrations to surf music without interference from killjoy 'squares'. At the same time, Roger Corman was tapping into a hipper young audience with his biker and psychedelic movies.

British musicals, which had hitherto been rather genteel adult affairs, all changed with US-born Richard Lester's two Beatles' movies, *A Hard Day's Night* (1964) and *Help!* (1965).

In 1973, George Lucas' *American Graffiti* sparked off a number of rites-of-passage pictures. In 1983, Francis Ford Coppola, Lucas' contemporary, shot two teen movies back to back, *The Outsiders* and *Rumble*

Fish, the first of which he called 'Gone With the Wind for kids', and the second 'an art film for kids'.

Perhaps the movies that most captured the Zeitgeist of the 1980s was the string of romantic youth comedies directed by John Hughes, dubbed 'the philosopher of adolescence' by critic Roger Ebert. The cycle began with *Sixteen Candles* (1984), which introduced several of the actors who would make up the director's stock company, known as the Brat Pack. Hughes' teenagers, like the hero of *Ferris Bueller's Day Off* (1986), defied the stifling bourgeois world with cheerful insouciance unlike the glum rebels of the past.

These cheery teen romances contrasted with the so-called 'gross out' movies: vulgar, raunchy comedies such as John Landis' *National Lampoon's Animal House* (1978) and Paul and Chris Weitz's *American Pie* (1999). Both strains of teen pic have continued in a similar manner into the 21st century.

KEY WORKS

↑ **American Graffiti**, 1973, GEORGE LUCAS
Paul Le Mat (left), Cindy Williams and Ron Howard in this dreamy vision of adolescent life in a small Californian town in 1962. Using rock 'n' roll hits of the day and with Haskell Wexler's brilliant hyperrealist cinematography, the film creates a golden past.

← **East of Eden**, 1955, ELIA KAZAN
James Dean as Cal, the misunderstood son of an unyielding father, finds sympathy and understanding from Julie Harris as Abra.

OTHER WORKS

Blackboard Jungle, 1955, BROOKS; Rebel Without A Cause, 1955, NICHOLAS RAY; Splendor in the Grass, 1961, KAZAN; A Hard Day's Night, 1964, LESTER; National Lampoon's Animal House, 1978, LANDIS; The Outsiders, 1983, COPPOLA; Sixteen Candles, 1984, HUGHES; The Breakfast Club, 1985, HUGHES; Ferris Bueller's Day Off, 1986, HUGHES; American Pie, 1999, WEITZ/WEITZ; Battle Royale, 2001, FUKASAKU

 Athleticism; Escapism; Musicalism; Eroticism; Cultism

 Expressionism; Avant-Gardism; Minimalism; Asian Minimalism; Experimentalism

THE SIXTIES
AND BEYOND
1960–

New Wavism

As the 1950s drew to a close, a radical change in the cinema took place, initially in France with the French New Wave (*La Nouvelle Vague*). By using unconventional filming methods and challenging received ideas, new wavism, which reacted against the hidebound *cinéma de papa* (dad's cinema), swept across continents.

ÉRIC ROHMER 1920–2010; ALAIN RESNAIS 1922–; JACQUES RIVETTE 1928–; AGNÈS VARDA 1928–; CLAUDE CHABROL 1930–; JEAN-LUC GODARD 1930–; FRANÇOIS TRUFFAUT 1932–84; LOUIS MALLE 1932–95; MILOŠ FORMAN 1932–; NAGISA ŌSHIMA 1932–; GLAUBER ROCHA 1938–81

hand-held cameras; improvisation; irreverence; location shooting; self-reflexivity; youth

As the 1960s dawned there was a new spirit abroad. Everywhere there was a battle between the old world and the new. In France, although Agnès Varda and Louis Malle could claim to have predated *La Nouvelle Vague*, it came into being when several young critics on the influential magazine *Cahiers du Cinéma* decided to take practical action in their battle against the *cinéma du papa* by making films themselves. Jean-Luc Godard (*Breathless*), François Truffaut (*The 400 Blows*), Alain Resnais (*Hiroshima, mon amour*), Eric Rohmer (*The Sign of Leo*), Jacques Rivette (*Paris Belongs To Us*) and Claude Chabrol (*Le beau Serge*), with their first films all made between 1959 and 1960, were reacting against the old-fashioned French cinema of boudoir comedies, swashbucklers and sterile star-studded adaptations of the classics.

Although the French New Wave directors differed in their approaches and sensibilities, there were many elements that united them: an irreverent, generally unsentimental treatment of character; episodic plots and deconstructed narratives; the use of hand-held cameras and lightweight equipment and a very small team; shooting in the streets and mostly in real locations, avoiding studios; jump cuts, eliminating the usual establishing shots, and elliptical cutting that drew attention to the relation between images and the medium itself; experimentation with filmic space and time; referential quotes from literature and favourite films as well as being self-reflexive; and a general existential attitude to society and to human behaviour.

The way the films were made reflected an interest in questioning cinema itself, by drawing attention to the conventions used in filmmaking. In this manner, the French New Wave directors strove to present an alternative to Hollywood by consciously breaking its conventions while at the same time paying homage to what they regarded as good in Hollywood cinema. Although the films represented a radical departure from traditional cinema and were aimed at a young intellectual audience, many of them achieved a measure of critical and financial success, gaining a wide audience both in France and abroad.

The *Nouvelle Vague*'s methods and subject matter were taken up and adapted by young directors in other countries, notably in the UK and Japan, and opened the way for the American indie movement. A short period of liberalisation of Eastern European countries in the Soviet bloc allowed some new wavism, especially in Czechoslovakia which produced an upsurge of imaginative films on contemporary themes using non-actors, minimal plots and a *cinéma vérité* (literally, 'camera truth') technique, Milos Forman's being the best examples. There were short-lived new waves

↑ **The 400 Blows (Les quatre cents coups),** 1959,
FRANÇOIS TRUFFAUT
Twelve-year-old Antoine Doinel (Jean-Pierre Léaud),
neglected by his mother and stepfather, plays truant,
takes to petty crime and ends up in reform school. There
was an extraordinary rapport between Truffaut and
Léaud, his alter ego, which was the start of a series of
films following Doinel through adolescence, marriage,
fatherhood and divorce.

in South America, too, particularly in Brazil
where a group called Cinema Novo, led by
Glauber Rocha, demonstrated a bold
revolutionary spirit in trying to create
indigenous work free from the pervading
North American influence. After 1968, the
experimental elements of the French New
Wave were already starting to become
assimilated into mainstream cinema.

OTHER WORKS
Le beau Serge, 1959, CHABROL; **The Sign of Leo,**
1959, ROHMER; **Hiroshima mon amour,** 1960, RESNAIS;
Paris Belongs to Us, 1960, RIVETTE; **Jules and Jim,**
1961, TRUFFAUT; **Cleo From 5 to 7,** 1962, VARDA; **Vivre
sa vie (It's My Life),** 1962, GODARD; **Loves of a
Blonde,** 1965, FORMAN; **Daisies,** 1966, CHITYLOVÁ;
The Diary of a Shinjuka Thief, 1968, ŌSHIMA;
Antonio das Mortes, 1969, ROCHA

KEY WORKS
Breathless (À bout de souffle), 1960,
JEAN-LUC GODARD [see p.108]
Amoral petty thief Michel Poiccard (Jean Paul
Belmondo), on the run for having killed a policeman,
has taken refuge in the Paris apartment of his
American girlfriend (Jean Seberg). In order to achieve
an immediacy in the performances, Godard cued the
actors, who were not allowed to learn their lines,
during the takes.

 Avant-Gardism; Italian Neo-Realism;
Auteurism; Postmodernism; American Indieism

 Monumentalism; Hollywood Studioism;
Escapism; Costume Romanticism; Classicism

The word *auteur* (author) was applied by young critics on the influential French magazine *Cahiers du Cinéma* to those film directors whose entire oeuvre can be seen as a personal statement in terms of style and theme, even those who worked within the studio system.

JOHN FORD 1894–1973; CARL DREYER 1889–1968; KENJI MIZOGUCHI 1898–1956; ALFRED HITCHCOCK 1899–1980; LUIS BUÑUEL 1900–83; MAX OPHÜLS 1902–57; ROBERT BRESSON 1901–99; AKIRA KUROSAWA 1912–98; MICHELANGELO ANTONIONI 1912–2007; INGMAR BERGMAN 1918–2007; FEDERICO FELLINI 1920–93; MIKLÓS JANCSÓ 1921–; PIER PAOLO PASOLINI 1922–75; JEAN-LUC GODARD 1930–; ANDREI TARKOVSKY 1932–86; KRZYSZTOF KIESLOWSKI 1941–96; WERNER HERZOG 1942–

director's cut; identifiable style and theme; individuality

In the first two decades of cinema, the general public was unaware of directors' names. People went to see a movie on the strength of stars or subject. Only a few directors became known because they were controversial, like DW Griffith, or made themselves visible, like Orson Welles, or became associated with a certain genre, like Cecil B DeMille and Alfred Hitchcock with the epic and thriller respectively. But, in the early 1950s, several young critics on *Cahiers du Cinéma* viewed the best filmmakers as having an individual

KEY WORKS

→ **The Seventh Seal,** 1957, INGMAR BERGMAN
Antonius Block (Max von Sydow, right), a 14th-century knight, returns from the Crusades to find Sweden ravaged by the plague. He then meets Death (Bengt Ekerot) with whom he plays a deadly game of chess in an attempt to save his life. This morality tale powerfully expresses Bergman's stark view of a godless universe.

and spontaneous stamp to their work, using the camera as a means of personal expression. They felt that the director should be considered in terms of thematic and stylistic consistency. This formulation shed light on those directors, especially in the Hollywood studio system, who had never been considered within the 'cinema-as-art' school of criticism. Among the critics' idols were Howard Hawks, Raoul Walsh and Nicholas Ray, who worked exclusively within the major studio system, and French directors Jean Renoir and Robert Bresson.

The seed was planted in 1948 by Alexandre Astruc in an article in the weekly *L'Ecran Français* entitled 'The Birth of the New Avant-Garde: Le Camera'. Astruc invented the term *camera stylo* (camera pen), and wrote of the cinema becoming 'a means of writing as supple and as subtle as that of written language', making a personal statement or describing a personal vision. It was François Truffaut, in the January 1954 issue of *Cahiers*, in the essay 'Une certaine tendance du cinéma français' ('a certain tendency in French cinema'), who coined the phrase *la politique des Auteurs*, later translated by American critic Andrew Sarris as 'the *auteur* theory'. Truffaut argued that, though a collective medium, a film always had the signature of the director on it, even the most menial in the Hollywood studio system.

In 1957, Truffaut wrote: 'The film of tomorrow appears to me even more personal than an individual and autobiographical novel … the film of tomorrow will not be directed by civil servants of the camera, but by artists … the film of tomorrow will resemble the person who made it.' In the late 1950s the *Cahiers du Cinéma* critics took the opportunity to become film *auteurs* themselves.

Soon the theory was taken up by critics all over the world and directors were given their dues as the principal creators of their films. With the growth of film studies and the increased knowledge of audiences, many movie-goers are today familiar with the names of great directors of the past, instantly recognisable by their style and content. For example, nobody could have directed *La Dolce Vita* (1960) other than Federico Fellini, or Ingmar Bergman *The Seventh Seal* (1957).

← **La Dolce Vita,** 1960, FEDERICO FELLINI
Anita Ekberg, as an American starlet, wanders tipsily into the Trevi Fountain. She is about to call out seductively to jaded gossip columnist Marcello Mastroianni to join her. This is one of the especially memorable setpieces in Fellini's vast panorama of decadent contemporary Roman society and is the film that introduced the expression 'paparazzi' into the English language.

OTHER WORKS
The Passion of Joan of Arc, 1928, DREYER; **Citizen Kane,** 1941, WELLES; **La ronde,** 1950, OPHÜLS; **Sansho the Bailiff,** 1954, MIZOGUCHI; **A Man Escaped,** 1956, BRESSON; **The Searchers,** 1956, FORD; **Vertigo,** 1958, HITCHCOCK; **L'avventura,** 1960, ANTONIONI; **Viridiana,** 1961, BUÑUEL; **The Roundup,** 1965, JANCSÓ; **Salo,** 1975, PASOLINI; **Stalker,** 1979, TARKOVSKY; **Ran,** 1985, KUROSAWA; **Three Colours: Blue,** 1993, **White,** 1994, **Red,** KIESLOWSKI

 Expressionism; Surrealism; Realism; Film Noirism; Minimalism

 Documentarism; Cartoonism; Teenagism; Dogmetism; Disasterism; FX-ism

● Eroticism in the cinema can be as suggestive as it is explicit. Unlike in pornography, the sex act and/or nudity is not a necessary component of it, but sex, not love or romance, is its main focus.

◐ **ERNST LUBITSCH** 1892–1947; **JOSEF VON STERNBERG** 1894–1969; **LUIS BUÑUEL** 1900–83; **INGMAR BERGMAN** 1918–2007; **ROGER VADIM** 1928–2000; **LOUIS MALLE** 1932–95; **NAGISA ÔSHIMA** 1932–; **BERNARDO BERTOLUCCI** 1940–; **PEDRO ALMODÓVAR** 1949–

◑ breaching of taboos; implicit or explicit sex scenes; subtle lighting

● More than any other subject, eroticism on the screen, in its various manifestations, has always been the prime target of puritans. In 1896, the Edison Manufacturing Company produced *The Kiss between May Irwin and John Rice*, which prompted a New York newspaper to write: 'Their unbridled kissing … is absolutely loathsome.' This first screen kiss caused calls

for censorship which eventually came about in the US with the restrictive Production Code (aka the Hays Code) in 1930. Gone were scantily clothed vamps like Theda Bara, Gloria Swanson, Jean Harlow and Clara Bow, and the salacious humour of Mae West was toned down. However, although the Code limited overt sexual portrayals, eroticism was still expressed by more subtle means.

The best Hollywood examples of post-Production Code eroticism were the cycle of films by Josef von Sternberg starring Marlene Dietrich as a femme fatale in the 1930s. As Europe was always far less narrow in its view of sexuality, American Louise Brooks had to go to Germany to play Lulu in GW Pabst's *Pandora's Box* (1929). With her black bobbed hair framing a kittenish face she became an icon of eroticism.

In most countries, screen sex was mainly put on hold during the Second World War, but resumed with greater vigour afterwards. In the US, any increase in sexual passion – such as the celebrated erotic beach scene between Burt Lancaster and Deborah Kerr in *From Here to Eternity* (1953), and Carroll Baker as the titillating virgin bride in *Baby Doll* (1956) – was accompanied by some public outrage. There was far more tolerance of eroticism in France at the same time with films such as Roger Vadim's *And God Created Woman* (1956), in which the director displayed the amoral charms of his 'sex kitten' wife (Brigitte Bardot), and Louis Malle's *The Lovers* (1958), an erotic satire which included a semi-nude love scene.

At the height of the counter-cultural and sexual revolution in the 1960s, explorations into eroticism went a step further. Spanish exile Luis Buñuel's witty and subversive *Belle de jour* (1967) contrasted with the Swedish Ingmar Bergman's *The Silence* (1963), though both contained certain scenes that were shocking at the time because of the unadorned frankness with which they were presented. Eroticism and notoriety continued to be linked with *succèss de scandale* such as Bernardo Bertolucci's portrayal of an exclusively physical relationship in *Last Tango in Paris* (1972), and Nagisa Ôshima's *In the Realm of the Senses* (*Ai No corrida*, 1976), which focused on obsessive sex between a gangster and a prostitute. Almost all taboos have been breached in the cinema, though the best erotic films have still managed, in most cases, to keep a distance, however narrow, from pornography.

KEY WORKS

Belle de jour, 1967, LUIS BUÑUEL
Catherine Deneuve, as the respectable wife of a doctor, spends her afternoons working, under the name of Belle de Jour, in a high-class brothel. This complex parable of social, sexual and emotional repression flits between dream and reality so that the spectator often wonders which is which, as in the still here.

In the Realm of the Senses (Ai No corrida),
1976, NAGISA ÔSHIMA
A married man (Tatsuya Fuji) and a geisha (Eiko Matsuda) retreat from the militarist Japan of 1936 into a world of their own where they obsessively act out their sexual fantasies in a quest for the ultimate orgasm. Exploring the link between eroticism and death, the film was an artistic breakthrough in the representation of explicit sex on screen.

OTHER WORKS

Pandora's Box, 1929, PABST; **Morocco,** 1930, VON STERNBERG; **From Here to Eternity,** 1953, ZINNEMANN; **And God Created Woman,** 1956, VADIM; **Baby Doll,** 1956, KAZAN; **The Lovers,** 1958, MALLE; **The Silence,** 1963, BERGMAN; **Last Tango in Paris,** 1972, BERTOLUCCI; **Tie Me Up Tie Me Down,** 1990, ALMODÓVAR; **Y tu mamá también (And Your Mother Too),** 2001, CUARÓN

 Exoticism; Naturalism; Film Noirism; New Wavism; Cultism

 Cartoonism; Propagandism; Socialist Realism; Racialism; Westernism

The majority of dystopian films are set in an uncertain future, under a repressive regime presented in nightmarish images. There are usually implicit and explicit references to contemporary society, the plots being cautionary tales on the possible consequences of our negative actions today.

FRITZ LANG 1890–1976; RIDLEY SCOTT 1937–; TERRY GILLIAM 1940–; JAMES CAMERON 1954–; LARRY WACHOWSKI 1965–; ANDY WACHOWSKI 1967–

bleakness; dehumanisation; futuristic sets; repressive regimes; retro noir; technology

Contrary to the feel-good hopefulness of much Hollywood fare, dystopian films provide a dominant vein of pessimism. However, despite the bleakness of existence under the all-powerful dictatorships depicted, the films often present a glimmer of hope, if not a complete reversal from Dystopia to Utopia. One of the major themes is the menace of rapidly advancing technology which has a dehumanising effect. Humankind is at the mercy of technology, rather than in control of it.

Films set in a dystopian society fall into different categories (though all contain warnings about the future): rule by an authoritarian elitist government; human societies ruled by aliens from another planet; societies ruled by a special group of powerful people – arch-villains, financiers and so on; post-apocalyptic societies trying to survive after, for example, a nuclear war; or society controlled by machines, robots etc. A subsection of the latter is cyberpunk, which is characterised by a focus on 'high tech and low life' where disillusioned loners exist in a world in which computers have a higher status than humans. A favourite genre in terms of style and plot is the film noir, transposed to a futuristic setting.

What is of prime importance is that the production design is convincing enough to evoke these societies. One of the earliest dystopian films, Fritz Lang's *Metropolis* (1927), an allegory of totalitarianism, is set in a futuristic city inspired by the New York skyline. To achieve the effects, lighting cameraman Eugen Schüfftan combined life-size action with models or artwork.

Metropolis set a precedent for many dystopian films including *Things To Come* (1936), designed and directed by William Cameron Menzies, and Ridley Scott's *Blade Runner* (1982). Jean Luc Godard's *Alphaville* (1965) was

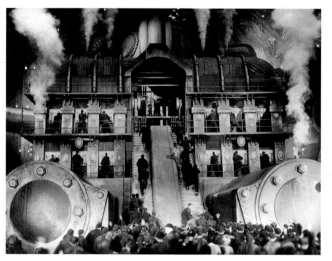

shot in a modern suburb of contemporary Paris standing in for the city where individualism and love have been suppressed, and a benign-seeming rural England was the setting for the book-burning society of François Truffaut's *Fahrenheit 451* (1966).

Chris Marker's *La jeteé* (1962), the inspiration behind Terry Gilliam's *Twelve Monkeys* (1995), is a 28-minute black-and-white post-Third World War story made up entirely of stills, except for one brief moving shot. Made previously, Gilliam's *Brazil* was an original dystopian vision.

As technology became even more essential, films, ironically using computer-generated imagery (CGI), reflected the anxiety of humans towards machines. In James Cameron's *The Terminator* (1984), humans struggle to free themselves from the control of intelligent cyborgs, and in Larry and Andy Wachowski's *The Matrix Trilogy: The Matrix* (1999), *The Matrix Reloaded* (2003) and *The Matrix Revolutions* (2003) humans are used 'as batteries for our evil robot insect overlords'.

KEY WORKS

↑ **Brazil,** 1985, TERRY GILLIAM
Jonathan Pryce as Sam Lowry, the Orwellian hero, a harassed clerk only kept sane by his vivid daydreams in contrast to the nightmarish 'reality' of his bizarre, alienating, highly bureaucratic environment. Here, he attempts to escape the police while facing 'imaginary' monsters.

← **Metropolis,** 1927, FRITZ LANG
The downtrodden factory workers, who live underground, mass beneath the giant machines belching smoke in rebellion against their masters. They have been made to rebel by a malign robot created in the image of a saintly girl (seen descending the stairs). The film pioneered the use of a futuristic dystopian society to comment on contemporary society.

OTHER WORKS
Things To Come, 1936, MENZIES; **1984 ,**1956, ANDERSON; **La jeteé,** 1962, MARKER; **Alphaville,** 1965, GODARD ; **Fahrenheit 451,** 1966, TRUFFAUT; **Soylent Green,** 1973, FLEISCHER ; **Logan's Run,** 1976, ANDERSON; **Mad Max,** 1979, MILLER; **Blade Runner,** 1982, RIDLEY SCOTT; **The Terminator,** 1984, CAMERON; **Twelve Monkeys,** 1995, GILLIAM; **The Matrix Trilogy:** 1999–2003, WACHOWSKI/WACHOWSKI

 Expressionism; Film Noirism; Postmodernism; Disasterism; FX-ism

 Constructivism; Costume Romanticism; Socialist Realism; Utopianism; Minimalism

When a movie is labelled a western, a musical, a film noir or a romantic comedy, preconceptions and expectations are automatically raised with audiences. Revisionist cinema reinterprets, challenges or even satirises traditional genres.

SAM PECKINPAH 1925–84; ROBERT ALTMAN 1925–2006; SERGIO LEONE 1929–89; CLINT EASTWOOD 1930–; RAINER WERNER FASSBINDER 1946–82; PEDRO ALMODÓVAR 1949–; JIM JARMUSCH 1953–; JOEL COEN 1955–; ETHAN COEN 1957–

anti-Establishment; cynical; demythological; self-reflexive

In Marxist politics, revisionism meant a move away from a revolutionary position to an evolutionary or reformist one. In the same way, revisionist films do not take a revolutionary stand against an accepted genre, but simply question its longstanding assumptions and make changes within it. Revisionist films, which derive from an affection and feeling for the genre, tend to be self-reflexive and self-conscious. In the more liberal 1960s, emerging filmmakers used the basic tenants of genre films for their own purposes, such as to expand their criticism of conservative values in society. The revisionist impulse appeared when myth had seemed to have overtaken reality, necessitating a reminder of forgotten principles.

The first films of the French New Wave directors were not immediately recognisable as 'art cinema'. François Truffaut, in his second feature, moved into gangster territory with *Shoot the Pianist* (1960), based on a David Goodis thriller. Jean-Luc Godard with *Breathless* (1960), dedicated to Monogram Pictures (the all-B movie studio), attempted to recapture (and comment on) the directness and economy of the American gangster movie. With *Une femme*

est une femme (*A Woman is a Woman*, 1961), Godard paid homage to the MGM musical and, in *Alphaville* (1965), he used the trappings of pulp fiction and film noir to tell a futuristic story.

Revisionist war films sought to desimplify attitudes to military conflict. Revisionist melodramas, of which Rainer Werner Fassbinder and Pedro Almodóvar were masters, unpicked the moral restrictions on them. The revisionist western generally favoured an anti-hero (often unglamorous and crude), stronger roles for women, and more sympathetic portrayals of both native and African Americans, and tended to be more violent and realistic. Sam Peckinpah's westerns like *Ride the High Country* (1962) and *The Wild Bunch* (1969) showed old-time cowboys ill at ease with the new-style West.

The Italian Sergio Leone, who took on the sacrosanct American genre of the western, branded it with his own style of amoral mythic grandeur. Clint Eastwood, who appeared in three Leone westerns, brought many of the revisionist elements of the spaghetti western into his own films as director, which demythologised the conventions of earlier westerns. Meanwhile, Czechoslovakia and East Germany lampooned the western from an Eastern European Communist perspective in *Lemonade Joe* (1964) and *Sons of the Great Bear* (1966) respectively.

Film noir, which already takes a bleak view of human nature, seemed less open to revisionism, but loosening constraints on sex and violence gave directors such as Robert Altman (*The Long Goodbye*, 1973), Roman Polanski (*Chinatown*, 1974), Curtis Hanson *LA Confidential* (1997) and the Coen Brothers in many of their films starting with *Blood Simple* (1984) a chance to further explore the genre in neo-noirs.

KEY WORKS

The Good, the Bad and the Ugly, 1966, SERGIO LEONE
Despite the film's title, none of the characters is good, though Clint Eastwood is bad and handsome as the monosyllabic, super-cool, poncho-clad, cheroot-chomping bounty hunter nicknamed 'Blondie'. With the stylised violence, the circular tracking shots, long silent close-ups, meaningful pauses and looks, Leone has attempted to create the apotheosis of the western.

Chinatown, 1974, ROMAN POLANSKI
In 1930s Los Angeles, Jack Nicholson as a Chandleresque private eye investigates a murky crime involving a corrupt tycoon and his daughter. In fact, Nicholson spends most of the movie with a white plaster on his nose as a result of a knifing by a nasty little hoodlum played by Polanski himself.

OTHER WORKS

Breathless (À bour de souffle), 1960, GODARD; **Shoot the Pianist**, 1960, TRUFFAUT; **Une femme est une femme (A Woman is a Woman)**, 1961, GODARD; **Ride the High Country**, 1962, PECKINPAH; **Lemonade Joe**, 1964, LIPSKÝ; **Alphaville**, 1965, GODARD; **Sons of the Great Bear**, 1966, MACH; **The Wild Bunch**, 1969, PECKINPAH; **Little Big Man**, 1970, PENN; **M*A*S*H**, 1970, ALTMAN; **The Bitter Tears of Petra Von Kant**, 1972, FASSBINDER; **The Long Goodbye**, 1973, ALTMAN; **Blood Simple**, 1984, COEN; **LA Confidential**, 1997, HANSON; **All About My Mother**, 1999, ALMODÓVAR; **The Man Who Wasn't There**, 2001, COEN

 Anti-Militarism; Liberalism; New Wavism; Postmodernism; Feminism

 Propagandism; Socialist Realism; Racialism; Classicism; Utopianism

An American independent (American indie) motion picture is generally financed and produced outside the direct control of a major Hollywood film studio. However, an indie is often made by established filmmakers and performers and distributed by one of the Hollywood studios, retaining full control of the material.

ROGER CORMAN 1926–; JOHN CASSAVETES 1929–89; DENNIS HOPPER 1935–2010; GEORGE ROMERO 1940–; DAVID LYNCH 1946–; GUS VAN SANT 1952–; JIM JARMUSCH 1953–; JOEL COEN 1954–; ETHAN COEN 1957–; SPIKE LEE 1957–; HAL HARTLEY 1959–; STEVEN SODERBERGH 1963–; QUENTIN TARANTINO 1963–; KEVIN SMITH 1970–

full control; genre-bending; low budgets; taboo subjects; youth

Many factors shaped the American indie film movement in the late 1960s and 1970s: the collapse of the studio system; the demise of the Production Code; audiences increasingly drawn from the 16 to 24 age bracket; and the counterculture of the Vietnam era. However, the notion of an independent cinema, made outside the traditional studio establishment, dates from as long ago as 1919 when four of the biggest names in motion pictures, DW Griffith, Charlie Chaplin, Mary Pickford and Douglas Fairbanks, formed United Artists, a move described at the time as 'the lunatics have taken over the asylum'.

In the 1930s and 1940s, the major studios consolidated their grip on the movie industry, however in the 1950s a number of independent producers broke the stranglehold of the majors. In fact, by 1958, 65 per cent of Hollywood movies were being made by independents. Roger Corman, 'King of the Z movie', and John

Cassavetes, whose *Shadows* (1959) was made for a mere $40,000, provided hope and inspiration for a new generation of directors, as did the French New Wave, who were turning their backs on conventional filming methods.

In the late 1960s, Hollywood found itself with an increasingly young audience. Dennis Hopper and Peter Fonda conceived, wrote, raised the finance for and starred in the alienated youth road movie *Easy Rider* (1969). Made for $400,000, the combination of drugs, rock music and violence caught the imagination of the young, and took more than $16 million at the box office. In an attempt to capture this audience, the major studios hired several young filmmakers (many of whom had been given their first break by Corman) and allowed them to make their films with relatively little studio control.

The field now opened for a new generation of independent directors, including David Lynch, Jim Jarmusch, Spike Lee, Hal Hartley, Gus van Sant and the Coen brothers, Joel and Ethan. The Coen's genre-bending style, alternating between spoofery and seriousness, had the greatest influence on the American indie movies that followed their debut feature, *Blood Simple* (1984). Quentin Tarantino unleashed his own visceral brand of cinephilia with *Reservoir Dogs* in 1992.

American indieism, which found its largest shop window at Robert Redford's Sundance Festival in Utah, developed rapidly into the 21st century, stimulated by affordable digital cinematography cameras. The borders between mainstream cinema and American indies, which came about as a reaction to the hypercapitalist mentality of studio filmmaking, gradually blurred, though the indies continued to represent the hip side of cinema.

KEY WORKS

↑ **Do The Right Thing,** 1989, SPIKE LEE
The racist Italian-American John Turturro (left) and Spike Lee, his employee as a pizza delivery boy, share a close moment in a film that confronted racial tensions without pretending to offer a conventional or pleasing resolution. Tapping a rich vein of street comedy, and shot in heavily saturated colours, the film owed little to Hollywood formulae or values.

↖ **Easy Rider,** 1969, DENNIS HOPPER
Two hippies, Dennis Hopper (left) with Peter Fonda, with the alcoholic southern lawyer Jack Nicholson along for the ride, hit the road in search of 'the real America' on their 'ultimate freedom machines'. What they find is mostly hostility towards them from small-town bigots. Hopper, who also directed, relied heavily on the expertise of cameraman László Kovács.

OTHER WORKS

Shadows, 1959, CASSAVETES; The Little Shop of Horrors, 1960, CORMAN; Night of the Living Dead, 1968, ROMERO; Eraserhead, 1977, LYNCH; Reservoir Dogs, 1982, TARANTINO; Blood Simple, 1984, COEN; Stranger Than Paradise, 1984, JARMUSCH; Sex, Lies, and Videotape, 1989, SODERBERGH; My Own Private Idaho, 1991, VAN SANT; Clerks, 1994, SMITH

 Teenagism; Auteurism; Cultism; Minimalism; Dogmetism

 Monumentalism; Hollywood Studioism; Costume Romanticism; Classicism; Racialism

Postmodernist cinema, in style, structure, plot, casting and technical vocabulary, generally looks back to various past forms and genres, blurring the lines between high and low culture. It is self-conscious and referential, relying on a shared film culture between the filmmakers and their audience.

WOODY ALLEN 1935–; **DAVID CRONENBERG** 1943–; **DAVID LYNCH** 1946–; **JEAN-JACQUES BEINEX** 1946–; **JOEL COEN** 1954–; **GUY MADDIN** 1956–; **ETHAN COEN** 1957–; **LUC BESSON** 1959–; **QUENTIN TARANTINO** 1963–; **TOM TYKWER** 1965–

intertextual; irony; parody; self-conscious; self-referential

According to Jean Baudrillard, the French guru of postmodernist theory, there are no originals, only copies or 'simulacra', images without a reference to any reality whatsoever. The interface between media and reality breaks down – we are as much part of the media as the media is part of us. This leads to self-conscious cinema of pastiche, and a recycling of images from the past, mimicking and mixing genres. The ironic inverted commas that inevitably cling to most postmodernist movies appeal especially to audiences steeped in American movie history. Each film contains elements that one expects from film noir, gangster movies, detective thriller or road movie, the boundaries being pushed as far as they can go, deconstructing conventional narratives.

Woody Allen's films often blur the limits between fiction and reality, often referencing Ingmar Bergman and Federico Fellini, while many of the films of the Coen brothers, Joel and Ethan, evoke the atmosphere of classic genre movies, sometimes quoting from specific ones obliquely. Their movies are fundamentally films noirs disguised as other genres. The Canadian director Guy Maddin reaches further back to German and Soviet silent films, and also to painting, classical music and literature, all merging with a postmodern sensibility. Another Canadian,

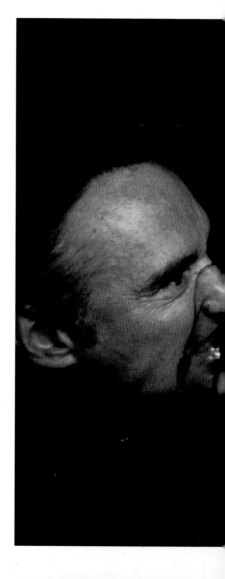

David Cronenberg, examined people at war with technology and their own perverse natures in an icy, almost abstract manner, turning the banal into nightmares.

In the 1980s, three young directors, Jean-Jacques Beinex, Luc Besson and Leos Carax,

KEY WORKS
↓ **Blue Velvet,** 1986, DAVID LYNCH
Gangster Dennis Hopper snorts gas through a mask and forces Isabella Rossellini, a nightclub singer, to have sex with him: a sadistic villain and a femme fatale, fundamental elements of film noir.

gave a new postmodern face to French cinema, deriving their aesthetic for their cool thrillers from commercials and pop videos. Tom Tykwer's *Run Lola Run* (1998) reinforces the randomness and meaninglessness of life, which is just a game. The plot revolves around three totally different outcomes to the same situation. This shows the postmodernist belief that everything is subjective and that there is no universal truth.

Ridley Scott's *Blade Runner* (1982)

where time and space have lost any meaningful parameters.

The dialogue of Quentin Tarantino's films, such as *Reservoir Dogs* (1992) and *Pulp Fiction* (1994), rely heavily on references to TV shows, pop music, B movies and celebrity gossip. Both are self-reflective studies of gangster movies as his *Inglourious Basterds* (2009) is of the war film, not war. Film noir is a favourite reference with its particular flavour of time and place. David Lynch's *Blue Velvet* (1986) absorbs the film noir imagery, using it as a satire on the complacency of small-town America, which turns back into a powerful parable of evil. Lynch, talking about *Wild At Heart* (1990) in *Time* magazine, said: 'See, I love 47 different genres in one film. And I love B-movies. But why not have three or four B's running together? Like a little hive!'.

← **Pulp Fiction,** 1994, QUENTIN TARANTINO
John Travolta and Uma Thurman take to the dance floor and twist to Chuck Berry's 'You Never Can Tell', a sequence that makes a direct reference to the dance in Jean-Luc Godard's *Bande a Part* (1964). Tarantino named his production company A Band Apart and drew on Godard's deconstruction of noir themes.

OTHER WORKS
Diva, 1981, BEINEX; **Blade Runner,** 1982, RIDLEY SCOTT; **Boy Meets Girl,** 1984, CARAX; **Subway,** 1985, BESSON; **Crimes and Misdemeanors,** 1989, ALLEN; **Wild At Heart,** 1990, LYNCH; **Reservoir Dogs,** 1992, TARANTINO; **The Big Lebowski,** 1998, COEN/COEN; **Run Lola Run,** 1998, TYKWER; **The Matrix,** 1999, WACHOWSKI/WACHOWSKI; **The Saddest Music in the World,** 2003, GUY MADDIN; **Inglourious Basterds,** 2009, TARANTINO

portrays a deconstructed world comprised of cityscapes reminiscent of Fritz Lang's *Metropolis* (1927), contemporary urban decay and futuristic technology such as the breakdown of the distinction between the human and the machine. It is a society

 Gangsterism; Film Noirism; New Wavism; Cultism; Revisionism

 Documentarism; Avant-Gardism; Realism; Experimentalism; Classicism

Dogme 95 was founded by the Danish directors Lars von Trier and Thomas Vinterberg as a reaction against commercial cinema and high budgets. The 1995 manifesto contained 10 rules by which Dogme (or Dogma) directors should abide in order to strip cinema down to its essentials.

SØREN KRAGH-JACOBSEN 1947–; LARS VON TRIER 1956–; KRISTIAN LEVRING 1957–; LONE SCHERFIG 1959–; JEAN-MARC BARR 1960–; SUSANNE BIER 1960–; THOMAS VINTERBERG 1969–; HARMONY KORINE 1973–

direct lighting and sound; hand-held cameras; low budget; manifesto; realism

Lars von Trier and Thomas Vinterberg drew up the Dogme 95 Manifesto, a so-called 'vow of chastity', with the intention of simplifying filmmaking by rejecting expensive and/or artificial settings and spectacular special effects, flashbacks and slow motion, postproduction modifications and fancy editing. The rules were as follows:

1 Filming must be done on location with no props or sets added

2 Only direct sound must be used. Music can only be used diegetically

3 The film must be shot with a hand-held camera;

4 The film must be in colour

5 Only direct light is to be used. Special lighting is not acceptable

6 Optical work and filters are forbidden

7 The action must be contemporary

8 Genre movies are not acceptable

9 The completed film must be transferred to Academy 35mm film, with an aspect ratio of 4:3, that is, not widescreen

10 The director must not be credited. 'I swear as a director to refrain from personal taste! I am no longer an artist. I swear to refrain from creating a "work", as I regard the instant as more important than the whole. My supreme goal is to force the truth out of my characters and settings. I swear to do so by all the means available and at the cost of any good taste and any aesthetic considerations.'

The majority of these rules were adhered to at the beginning, certainly the breaching of 'good taste', although the anonymity of the director was never retained. The first two Dogme films, shown at the 1998 Cannes Film Festival, were Vinterberg's *The Celebration* and von Trier's *The Idiots*. There followed Søren Kragh-Jacobsen's *Mifune* (1999), Kristian Levring's *The King Is Alive* (2000), Lone Scherfig's *Italian for Beginners* (2000) and Susanne Bier's *Open Hearts* (2002).

There were a few non-Danish directors who signed up to the Manifesto, such as the American Harmony Korine (*Julien Donkey-Boy*, 1999), the French-American Jean-Marc Barr (*Lovers*, 1999), the Korean Hyuk Byun (*Interview*, 2000) and the Argentinean José Luis Marquès (*Fuckland*, 2000). Most of their films had a feeling of freshness and playfulness about them and were successful. Gradually, however, the Dogme 95 Manifesto, which was originally a kind of homage to François Truffaut's influential 1954 essay 'Une certaine tendance du cinéma français' in the French film magazine *Cahiers du Cinéma*, became a reference rather than a rule book. In fact, sets, artificial lighting, non-diegetic sound and so on started to be used more and more, especially by von Trier (*Dogville*, 2003) and Vinterberg (*Dear Wendy*, 2005). Gus Van Sant revived much of its spirit with a few of his films.

KEY WORKS

↑ **The Idiots**, 1998, LARS VON TRIER
The birthday orgy when all of the members of a commune strip off. The anti-bourgeois group's goal is to embrace what they term their 'inner idiots' by pretending to be mentally disabled, behaving in a socially unacceptable manner in public. Keeping strictly to the Dogme rules, the film is purposefully provocative in both style and substance.

← **The Celebration**, 1998, THOMAS VINTERBERG
Danish patriarch Helge Klingenfeldt (Henning Moritzen) at the family gathering for his 60th birthday, is alone with his thoughts, separated from the blurred others, while dark and painful secrets hang over the celebration.

OTHER WORKS
Julien Donkey-Boy, 1999, KORINE; **Lovers,** 1999, BARR; **Mifune,** 1999, KRAGH-JACOBSEN; **Fuckland,** 2000, MARQUES; **Interview,** 2000, BYUN; **Italian for Beginners,** 2000, SCHERFIG; **The King Is Alive,** 2000, LEVRING; **Gerry,** 2002, VAN SANT; **Open Hearts,** 2002, BIER; **Dogville,** 2003, VON TRIER; **Dear Wendy,** 2005, VINTERBERG

 Realism; New Wavism; American Indiesm; Minimalism; Postmodernism

 Illusionism; Monumentalism; Hollywood Studioism; Auteurism; Classicism

From the 1970s a string of films was released featuring stellar casts threatened by earthquakes, sinking ships, fires, air crashes and other catastrophes, carrying the optimistic message that survival in all circumstances is possible.

ISHIRŌ HONDA 1911–93; RONALD NEAME 1911–; IRWIN ALLEN 1916–91; JOHN GUILLERMIN 1925–; WOLFGANG PETERSEN 1941–; JAMES CAMERON 1954–; ROLAND EMMERICH 1955–

heroism; large casts; multiple plot lines; special effects;

Natural or man-made disasters have been the subject of films since the silent days, providing catharsis for audiences. While the spectacular disaster is central to the films, using the latest special effects, they concentrate on its consequences, the surrounding events, and the heroic efforts for survival of ordinary men and women. This requires many plot lines and multiple characters, with the casting of well-known stars helping to make identification immediate.

The disasters can be divided into three main types: natural disasters (earthquakes, tidal waves and so on), disasters caused by technology failing, or by changes in the environment or the creation of monsters, and disasters caused by terrorism or enemy or alien powers.

The earliest disaster movies came out of the desire to demonstrate the epic possibilities of silent cinema. Italy produced two versions of *The Last Days of Pompei* with much improved special effects between 1913 and 1926. The former predated DW Griffith's *Intolerance* (1916), which depicted the fall of Babylon in the most graphic and spectacular manner.

The first real wave of disaster movies came between the wars, in the 1930s, with

films such as *King Kong* (1933), John Ford's *The Hurricane* (1937), *San Francisco* (1936), culminating in a vast earthquake, and *In Old Chicago* (1937) ending with the great fire. The beginning of the Atomic Age influenced the science-fiction films of the 1950s, which used the menace of nuclear disaster as plot points, including, understandably, several Japanese productions, the most famous being *Godzilla* (1954) and its many spin-offs.

Unlike the futuristic films of the 1950s, disaster movies in the 1970s often dealt with more familiar situations, such as fires in buildings and air crashes, the latter related to the vast increase in air travel from the mid-1960s. The huge box-office success of *Airport* (1970), in which an airliner comes under threat from a bomb, spawned three sequels and the spoof *Airplane!* (1980). It also initiated a cycle of disaster movies that included *Earthquake* (1974), a film made in Sensurround that gave audiences the sensation of a minor tremor at certain climactic moments. Producer-director Irwin Allen, dubbed 'The

Master of Disaster', gave us *The Poseidon Adventure* (1972) and *The Towering Inferno* (1974), two of the best of the genre.

With the rise of computer-generated imagery (CGI) combined with pre-millennium fears, from the mid-1990s there was a revival of disaster movies. The ability to mix live action with digital technology increased the effect of such films as *Independence Day* (1996), *Titanic* (1997), *Armageddon* (1998), *The Day After Tomorrow* (2004), *Poseidon* (2006) – a remake by Wolfgang Petersen – and a further doomsday scenario with Roland Emmerich's *2012* (2009).

KEY WORKS

 The Towering Inferno, 1974, JOHN GUILLERMIN, IRWIN ALLEN

Eerily prescient, this shows the blazing special effects of a burning San Francisco skyscraper, ignited during its opening ceremony, attended by several superstars, each hoping to be saved by daring fire chief Steve McQueen. The film won Oscars for Best Editing, Best Cinematography and Best Song.

 Titanic, 1997, JAMES CAMERON

Young lovers, poor artist Leonardo DiCaprio, from steerage, and Kate Winslet, rich girl in First Class, make their treacherous way together through the flooded ballroom as the ship sinks deeper and deeper. The ship, in this 194-minute, $200 million film, was constructed from large and small models, visual effects and computer animation.

OTHER WORKS

The Last Days of Pompeii, 1913, CASERINI; Intolerance, 1916, GRIFFITH; King Kong, 1933, COOPER/SCHOEDSACK; San Francisco, 1936, VAN DYKE; In Old Chicago, 1937, KING; The Hurricane, 1937, FORD; Godzilla, 1954, HONDA; The Day the Earth Caught Fire, 1961, GUEST; Airport, 1970, SEATON; The Poseidon Adventure, 1972, NEAME/ALLEN; Earthquake, 1974, ROBSON; Airplane!, 1980, ABRAHAMS/ZUCKER/ZUCKER; Independence Day, 1996, EMMERICH; Armageddon, 1998, BAY; The Perfect Storm, 2000, PETERSEN; The Day After Tomorrow, 2004, EMMERICH; Poseidon, 2006, PETERSEN; 2012, 2009, EMMERICH;

Illusionism; Monumentalism; Hollywood Studioism; Dystopianism; FX-ism

Utopianism; Avant-Gardism; Experimentalism; New Wavism; Minimalism

The cult movie is any film that for reasons unallied to its intrinsic artistic quality has attracted obsessive devotion from a group of fans. Cult films are usually offbeat, camp and outrageous with one-dimensional characters and extravagant plots.

RUSS MEYER 1922–2004; ED WOOD JR 1924–78; ALEJANDRO JODOROWSKY 1929–; MONTE HELLMAN 1932–; JOHN WATERS 1946–

bad taste; camp; cheap; eccentric; extravagant characters and plots; garish sets; offbeat

Many cult movies cut across film genres, although horror or sci-fi movies are favourites. Some were flops on their first release, but then achieved cult status later on when seen in a different light. For example, when *Reefer Madness* (1936), a propaganda film made by a religious group to warn against the dangers of marijuana, was re-released in 1972, it became a cult hit, especially among the pot-smoking young – the very people it had aimed to alarm.

The most passionate fans see the films dozens of times until they can repeat the dialogue. *The Rocky Horror Picture Show* (1975), combining the conventions of science fiction, musicals and horror films with elements of transvestism and homosexuality, attracted fans dressed as characters from the film to midnight screenings. Since 1999, a sing-a-long version of *The Sound of Music* (1965) has played to packed houses all over the English-speaking world. It is an interactive entertainment in which audiences, dressed as nuns and Nazis, sing all the songs with the help of subtitles.

The expression 'so bad it's good' is often used to describe many cult movies. For example, Ed Wood Jr gathered a cult following for being considered one of the worst directors of all time. So cheap were Wood's films that the spaceships in *Plan 9 From Outer Space* (1958) were represented by spinning hubcaps and paper plates. Wood's *Glen or Glenda* (1953) is a hilariously well-meaning film on transvestism presented as an educational

– and liberally splattered with blood, nudity and violence.

Similarly, Werner Herzog's *Aguirre, the Wrath of God* (1972) has a fanatical following because of its allegory of colonialism, its pictorial flair and the mesmerising, verging on hammy performance by Klaus Kinski. Another highly regarded cult film, Monte Hellman's low-budget *Two-Lane Blacktop* (1971) – about two car freaks who race across America challenging others along the way – combines an existential character study with exciting car chases.

KEY WORKS

 El Topo, 1970, ALEJANDRO JODOROWSKY
'I ask of cinema what most North Americans ask of psychedelic drugs,' Jodorowsky stated. Strikingly photographed against a dramatically beautiful desert landscape, the film tells of a journey taken by a gunfighter known as El Topo (Jodorowsky, back to camera) who meets an armless man sitting on the shoulders of a legless man.

 The Rocky Horror Picture Show, 1975, JIM SHARMAN
Tim Curry as Dr Frank-N-Furter, the 'sweet transvestite from Transsexual, Transylvania', with Patricia Quinn (centre) as Magenta, the maid, Richard O'Brien (who wrote the original stage musical) as Riff-Raff, and Nell Campbell (left) as, a groupie, in a typical outrageously camp number.

OTHER WORKS
Reefer Madness, 1936, GASNIER; Glen or Glenda, 1953, WOOD; Plan 9 From Outer Space, 1958, WOOD; The Sound of Music, 1965, WISE; Faster Pussycat! Kill! Kill!, 1965, MEYER; Two-Lane Blacktop, 1971, HELLMAN; Aguirre, the Wrath of God, 1972, HERZOG; Pink Flamingos, 1972, WATERS; The Wicker Man, 1973, HARDY; This is Spinal Tap, 1984, REINER; Withnail and I, 1987, BRUCE ROBINSON

documentary but interrupted, from time to time, by a ranting and raving Bela Lugosi. Russ Meyer's 'nudie-cutie' films also gained a cult following, especially *Faster Pussycat! Kill! Kill!* (1965). Gaining more of a following among gay audiences was John Waters' *Pink Flamingos* (1972) featuring drag superstar Divine. Occasionally more mainstream films catch the imagination of a group of fans, such as *This is Spinal Tap* (1984), Rob Reiner's 'mockumentary' send-up of the rock industry; Bruce Robinson's acidly witty *Withnail and I* (1987) about two 'resting' young actors in the 1960s; and Robin Hardy's *The Wicker Man* (1973), a British horror film about a Scottish police officer who gets caught up in Celtic pagan rituals when visiting an isolated island to search for a missing girl.

Alejandro Jodorowsky's *El Topo* (1970) has the perfect recipe for cultists: religious symbolism – Christian, Buddhist and pagan

Exoticism; Emotionalism; Musicalism; Teenagism; Postmodernism

Documentarism; Realism; Experimentalism; Classicism; Minimalism

Minimalism

🕐 Minimalism generally refers to a type of avant-garde cinema, whether documentary or fiction, that reduces to a bare minimum subject matter, editing, film technique and equipment.

◑ ROBERT BRESSON 1907–99; JEAN-MARIE STRAUB 1933–; DANIÈLE HUILLET 1936–2006; THEO ANGELOPOULOS 1936–; ABBAS KIAROSTAMI 1940–; RAINER WERNER FASSBINDER 1945–82; BÉLA TARR 1955–; AKI KAURISMÄKI 1957–; CARLOS REYGADAS 1971–

◓ diegetic music; long takes; minimum editing; simplicity; small crew; static

● Minimalist cinema can best be illustrated at its extremes, such as Andy Warhol's black-and-white and silent 'anti-films', for example *Sleep* (1963) or *Empire* (1964). The films are projected not at the standard sound speed of 24 frames per second, but at silent speed – 16 frames per second – drawing out the action to seem even more minimal.

Perhaps the father of minimalism is Robert Bresson, whose austere, uncompromising and elliptical oeuvre was impressively consistent and inspirational since *Diary of a Country Priest* (1950), which used non-actors and non-emotional acting, natural and direct sound.

Theo Angelopoulos is a master of the long take and slow pans that he uses in ambitious allegories of Greek politics and metaphysical road movies like *Eternity and a Day* (1998). The husband-and-wife team of Jean-Marie Straub and Danièle Huillet used voice-overs, amateur performers reading texts without emotion, and extremely long takes, either with a fixed camera or in complex tracking shots. Many such directors expect audiences to commit to more intense levels of concentration and engagement necessary to gain the rewards that this kind of contemplative cinema offers.

In the area of narrative films, the German Rainer Werner Fassbinder developed rapid working methods and was able to complete as many as four or five films per year on extremely low budgets in the early 1970s. The first of his movies were austere and

fragmented, extensions of his work in the theatre, and shot usually with static camera and with deliberately unnaturalistic dialogue. In Hungary, Béla Tarr, who cites Fassbinder as his greatest influence, created a cinema of long takes, sometimes more than 11 minutes, though the camera here is seldom static.

The Finn Aki Kaurismaki's films about taciturn losers in bleak surroundings are enlivened by his dry humour. Of an even younger generation is the Mexican Carlos Reygadas, noted for the formal rigour of his strange narratives that owe as much to Luis Buñuel as to Robert Bresson.

Both Iranian and Romanian cinema fall into the minimalist category, inspired to a certain extent by Italian neo-realism. Leading Iranian director Abbas Kiarostami's films became more and more reductionist after his minimalist masterpieces of the 1990s such as *Through the Olive Trees* (1994). *Ten* (2002) consists of 10 takes in close-up of different women in a car; and *Shirin* (2008), which shows a group of women photographed in an audience ostensibly watching a film of a 14th-century Persian tale. We watch their reactions and only hear the soundtrack of the film, using their expressions to help us imagine the story.

Cristi Puiu's *The Death of Mr Lazerescu* (2005) was the start of the Romanian new wave films – almost documentary-like observations of Romanian society with an underlying vein of black humour and a minimum use of music.

↑ **Diary of a Country Priest,** 1950, ROBERT BRESSON
Claude Laydu as a young priest trying to bring comfort to his parishioners, even to a spiteful girl (Nicole Ladmiral). Through pared-down images, real locations and a first-person narrative, Bresson manages to convey the inner anguish of the characters.

OTHER WORKS

Sleep, 1963, WARHOL; Empire, 1964, WARHOL; Not Reconciled, 1965, STRAUB; The Merchant of Four Seasons, 1971, WERNER FASSBINDER; Stranger Than Paradise, 1984, JARMUSCH; Satantango, 1994, TARR; Through the Olive Trees, 1994, KIAROSTAMI; The Werckmeister Harmonies, 2000, TARR; Japón, 2002, REYGADAS; The Man Without a Past, 2002, AKI KAURISMÄKI; Ten, 2002, KIAROSTAMI; Five Dedicated to Ozu, 2003, KIAROSTAMI; The Death of Mr Lazerescu, 2005, PUIU; 4 Months, 3 Weeks and 2 Days, 2007, MUNGIU; Shirin, 2008, KIAROSTAMI

KEY WORKS

← **Eternity and a Day,** 1998, THEO ANGELOPOULOS
Alexandre (Bruno Ganz), a dying poet, spends his last day with his memories and a young Albanian refugee boy (Achileas Skevis). Using long takes and reverse tracking, Angelopoulos creates a fusion of reality and dreams, a visual metaphor for the isolation of the soul.

 Avant-Gardism; Realism; American Indieism; Dogmetism; Asian Minimalism

 Monumentalism; Hollywood Studioism; Escapism; Costume Romanticism; Classicism

After the death of Yasujiro Ozu, the great Japanese master of *shomin-geki* (contemporary lives of ordinary people), it seemed that his singular minimalist oeuvre deterred followers. However, in the late 20th and early 21st century, a number of Asian directors gained inspiration from it.

YASUJIRO OZU 1903–63; HOU HSIAO-HSIEN 1947–; EDWARD YANG 1947–2007; TSAI MING-LIANG 1957–; HONG SANG SOO 1960–; ANH HUNG TRAN 1962–; HIROKAZU KORE-EDA 1962–; APICHATPONG WEERASETHAKUL 1970–; ZHANG KE JIA 1970–

'empty' frame; long takes; muted action; slender plot; static camera; understated acting

There were two main genres in Japanese cinema: *jidai-geki* (period films) and *gendai-geki* (contemporary settings) with its sub-genre of *shomin-geki* (about lower- and middle-class family life).

Yasujiro Ozu, in particular, was the prime exponent of the latter. All of his post-Second World War films are about middle-class family relationships told through the traditional Japanese concept of 'sympathetic sadness'. He had no interest in plots. It was the interplay of characters that absorbed him. He kept exteriors to a minimum, never used a dissolve, and the camera seldom moved, being fixed about a metre from the floor at the level of the eyes of the seated actors. His long takes, sometimes 'empty' shots, were often punctuated by short exterior shots and intensified by music.

Although stylistically less restrictive, many of the younger Asian directors, not only Japanese, followed the spirit and the basic minimalistic principles of Ozu. For example, the Japanese Hirokazu Kore-Eda and the Taiwanese Hou Hsiao-Hsien have dedicated two of their films, *Still Walking* (2008) and *Café Lumière* (2005), respectively, to Ozu.

Most of the disciples of Ozu, and other masters of *shomin-geki* such as Mikio Naruse and Heinosuke Gosho, shared their surface simplicity and hidden structural complexity, though their narratives tend to be more cryptic and elliptical. Like the more recent films of 2006 by Hou Hsiao-Hsien (*Three Times*) and Zhang Ke Jia (*Still Life*), pivotal plot moments take place outside the frame or between two static scenes, leaving the audience to infer action, while any dramatic climaxes are played down. Relationships are examined by what is unspoken rather than expressed. There are few close-ups and the pacing is deliberate.

Despite the new Asian minimalists coming from different countries: Hong Sang Soo (South Korea), Zhang Ke Jia (China), Edward Yang (Taiwan), Anh Hung Tran (Vietnam), Apichatpong Weerasethakul (Thailand) and Tsai Ming-Liang (Malaysia), they differ in their styles and preoccupations, though failed romantic

relationships seem to dominate. They do, however, share one stylistic device – the long take.

In *What is Cinema?* (1958), André Bazin wrote: 'Thanks to the depth of field, whole scenes are covered in one take, the camera remaining motionless. Dramatic effects for which we had formerly relied on montage were created out of the movements of the actors within a fixed framework.' Bazin believed the long take allowed for greater realism, and encouraged a more active mental attitude on the part of the viewer, who could now explore more fully the interpretive and moral ambiguity inherent in the film image. Bazin would have heartily approved of the new Asian minimalism.

KEY WORKS

Three Times, 2006, HOU HSIAO-HSIEN
Qi Shu as May the hostess of a pool hall in the first of three love stories, which takes place in 1966. She is courted by Chen (Chang Chen), a young man about to report for military service. The room is perfectly framed and lit as May, indifferent to Chen, goes about her work. (The other stories, played by the same two leads, are set in 1911 and 2005).

Still Life, 2006, ZHANG KE JIA
Set in the region of the Yangtze river where millions of Chinese are being displaced for the building of a hydro-electric dam, Shen (Tao Zhao), a nurse, while searching for her husband, meets archaeologist Wang (Hongwei Wang) amid the destruction. With austerely beautiful long takes, Jia watches a thousand years of history being demolished in the name of industry.

OTHER WORKS

Platform, 2000, JIA; **Vertical Ray of the Sun,** 2000, HUNG TRAN; **Yi Yi,** 2000, YANG; **What Time is it Over There,** 2001, MING-LIANG; **Tropical Malady,** 2004, WEERASETHAKUL; **Woman is the Future of Man,** 2004, SANG SOO; **Café Lumière,** 2005, HSIAO-HSIEN; **Still Walking,** 2008, KORE-EDA

 Realism; Orientalism; Dogmetism; Minimalism; American Indieism

 Monumentalism; Constructivism; Costume Romanticism; Hollywood Studioism

🕐 Feminism in the cinema attempted to criticise and redress the main image of women as little more than objects of desire ever since Theda Bara appeared as a 'vamp' in 1915.

⬤ **ALICE GUY** 1873–1968; **GERMAINE DULAC** 1882–1942; **MARGUERITE DURAS** 1914–96; **INGMAR BERGMAN** 1918–2007; **SATYAJIT RAY** 1921–92; **AGNÈS VARDA** 1928–; **PEDRO ALMODÓVAR** 1949–; **CHANTAL AKERMAN** 1950–; **JANE CAMPION** 1954–; **JAFAR PANAHI** 1960–; **SAMIRA MAKHMALBAF** 1977–

🕐 female dilemmas; female protagonists; gender equality

⬤ As films and the film industry changed radically in the 1960s so did film criticism, which involved a general revaluation of morality in cinema. Reflecting the various liberation movements: Marxist, 'queer', Freudian, black and feminist film criticism grew in importance. The latter looked at how women have been portrayed in the movies, concentrating on the negative stereotyping of women characters, which categorised them as dumb blondes, femmes fatales, bitches, mothers and whores – all seen as ways of putting women in their place in a patriarchal society.

Feminist critics argued that the majority of films presented women only in their relation to men. According to Budd Boetticher, a director of westerns: 'What counts is what the heroine provokes, or rather what she represents. In herself the woman has not the slightest importance.'

Action was identified with masculinity. As Jean-Luc Godard once famously said: 'All you need to make a movie is a girl and a gun.' Man was the subject, woman the object. Scopophilia, literally, 'the love of looking', was a word some feminist critics used to describe the way women's bodies were the objects of the male gaze and male desire. They complained that the voyeuristic nature of predominantly mainstream cinema got audiences to identify with the male protagonist. However, there is a certain

acknowledgement of the strong female characters, played by Joan Crawford, Bette Davis and Barbara Stanwyck in the Hollywood 'women's pictures' of the 1940s and 1950s, and Howard Hawks' women in traditionally male settings.

There is an ambiguity in films by directors such as the heterosexual Ingmar Bergman, where the female face in close-up is at the centre of his field of vision, and homosexuals Rainer Werner Fassbinder and Pedro Almodóvar, where women are sometimes portrayed as elements of camp. There is no ambiguity in the attitudes to women by directors as distinctly different as Carl Dreyer and Satyajit Ray, but they are both at ease in presenting independently minded women, as in the latter's *Charulata* (*The Lonely Wife*, 1964).

Feminist critics helped change certain entrenched attitudes and more films became less sexist, even to the extent of having feminist themes in commercial cinema. The increase of women filmmakers over the years, worldwide, has also helped redress the balance, among them Gillian Armstrong and Jane Campion from Australia and New Zealand respectively. France, more than most countries, produced a relatively large amount of women directors starting with Alice Guy, the world's first female director, who began making films in 1900, and continuing with Germaine Dulac and on to Marguerite Duras and Agnès Varda. Some of the most feminist directors have, ironically, come from Iran, one of the least feminist countries. These include Jafar Panahi (*The Circle*, 2000), and the Makhmalbaf family: Mohsen (father), Marzieh Meshkini (mother), Samira and Hana (daughters).

KEY WORKS

↑ **The Circle,** 2000, JAFAR PANAHI
Banned in Iran, the film shows that under current Iranian law, unattached women are made to feel like hunted animals, suggesting that they are in prison, both figuratively and literally. Even here in a phone booth, a mother feels trapped and spied upon as she informs her family that her daughter has given birth to a girl and fears angry reprisals from the in-laws.

← **Charulata (The Lonely Wife),** 1964, SATYAJIT RAY
Charulata (Madhabi Mukherjee), the bored and neglected wife of an intellectual journalist, falls in love with Amal (Soumitra Chatterjee), a young poet and her husband's cousin. This scene, where she begins to swing higher and higher as Amal sits writing, suggests a sexuality rare in the context of Indian cinema.

OTHER WORKS
The Smiling Madame Beudet, 1923, DULAC; **Master of the House,** 1925, DREYER; **His Girl Friday,** 1940, HAWKS; **Gertrud,** 1964, DREYER; **Persona,** 1966, BERGMAN; **Jeanne Dielman, 23 Quai du Commerce, 1080 Bruxelles,** 1975, AKERMAN; **One Sings, The Other Doesn't,** 1977, VARDA; **The Marriage of Maria Braun,** 1978, FASSBINDER; **Women on the Verge of a Nervous Breakdown,** 1988, ALMODÓVAR; **An Angel at My Table,** 1990, CAMPION ; **The Day I Became a Woman,** 2000, MEZKINI; **Ten,** 2002, KIAROSTAMI; **At Five in the Afternoon,** 2003, MAKHMALBAF

 Costume Romanticism; Anti-Militarism; Film Noirism; Emotionalism; Liberalism

 Athleticism; Horrorism; Racialism; Westernism; Eroticism

Special effects (abbreviated variously as FX, SFX or EFX), which depend on technology as much as artistry, have advanced further than any other branch of film. But the essential aim has always been to manufacture illusions that are impossible to film without trickery.

GEORGES MÉLIÈS 1861–1938; CECIL B DEMILLE 1881–1959; WILLIS O'BRIEN 1886–1962; JOHN P FULTON 1902–66; ISHIRÔ HONDA 1911–93; RAY HARRYHAUSEN 1920–; STANLEY KUBRICK 1928–99; DOUGLAS TRUMBULL 1942–; GEORGE LUCAS 1944–; STEVEN SPIELBERG 1946–; JAMES CAMERON 1954–; TIM BURTON 1958–; PETER JACKSON 1961–

computer-generated imagery; matte paintings; motion control; trick photography

There are two kinds of special effects: optical or photographic effects which are achieved by manipulating the film image; and physical effects achieved through the use of mechanical devices on set. Optical effects include computer-generated imagery (CGI), digital compositing, digital matte paintings, green screen technology, miniatures, morphing and travelling mattes. Physical effects include animatronic puppets, full-scale mockups, and rain, storm and snow machines. A complicated FX sequence may include a variety of visual and mechanical effects.

The names of pioneers of FX, like Willis O'Brien, who helped conceive the first *King Kong* (1933), his disciple Ray Harryhausen, John P Fulton and Douglas Trumbull, who was special photographic effects supervisor on Stanley Kubrick's *2001: A Space Odyssey* (1968), have gradually become known to the general public. Without figures such as this, Cecil B DeMille would never have been

able to part the Red Sea in *The Ten Commandments* (1956) nor Ishirô Honda create his monsters such as *Godzilla*, nor Tim Burton to realise the first two *Batman* movies nor Peter Jackson's CGI-dominated spectacles.

The French conjuror and inventor Georges Méliès could be said to be the originator of special effects. In 1898, the shutter of his camera jammed while he was filming a street scene. This incident made him realise the potential of trick photography to create magical effects. In fact, Méliès used stop-motion photography, multiple exposure, matting, animation and the dissolve.

The UFA studios in Berlin produced some of the most advanced visual effects of the silent era, notably FW Murnau's *Faust* (1926) and Fritz Lang's *Metropolis* (1927). In the latter, lighting cameraman Eugen Schüfftan combined life-size action with models and artwork. The term 'special effects' was first used in the same year to credit the mechanical effects in Raoul Walsh's *What Price Glory?* (1926), but it took another 13 years before FX was recognised by the Academy Awards, the first being given to *The Rains Came* (1939) for the impressive recreation of an earthquake and floods by technician Fred Sersen. Many of the techniques in the film, such as weather machines, miniatures and matte paintings, continued to be used for the next decades. A matte painting was less costly than filming with live actors such as in a convent high up in the Himalayas (*Black Narcissus*, 1947) or on Mount Rushmore (*North By Northwest*, 1959), giving the illusion of on-location shooting.

The blending of cartoon and live characters, something that dates from the silent era, was given a boost by computer technology, most evident in *Who Framed*

Roger Rabbit? (1988). Because of the advances of computer technology, back projection and brush and canvas matte paintings, and even animatronics, used for the shark in *Jaws* (1975), have become less and less used. Green screens placed behind actors that allow CGI to be integrated into the scene have largely replaced blue screens because green provides finer outlines. CGI is now used with such great frequency especially in blockbusters that the human element in films is often overwhelmed.

KEY WORKS

→ King Kong, 1933, MERIAN C COOPER, ERNEST B SCHOEDSACK [see overleaf]
Bruce Cabot rescues Fay Wray from Kong's mountain lair in a scene that uses matte processes and stop-motion photography – shooting one frame at a time. Although the gargantuan ape appears huge, Kong was a 46-centimetre model.

↑ 2001: A Space Odyssey, 1968, STANLEY KUBRICK
Keir Dullea as astronaut Dr David Bowman goes about his daily routine of checking the spaceship. But he is merely a machine controlled by a machine: the HAL 9000 computer. Ironically, the film that wryly condemns a hyper-technological future is a high-tech product in itself not far behind the futuristic world it predicts.

OTHER WORKS
Die Niebelungen (Siegfried and Kriemhild's Revenge), 1924, LANG; Faust, 1926, MURNAU; Metropolis, 1927, LANG; What Price Glory?, 1926, WALSH; The Rains Came, 1939, BROWN; Black Narcissus, 1947, POWELL/PRESSBURGER; North By Northwest, 1959, HITCHCOCK; Jaws, 1975, SPIELBERG; Star Wars, 1977, LUCAS; The Fly, 1986, CRONENBERG; Who Framed Roger Rabbit?, 1988, ZEMECKIS; Batman, 1989, BURTON; Jurassic Park, 1993, SPIELBERG; Lord of the Rings, 2001, JACKSON; Avatar, 2009, CAMERON

 Illusionism; Expressionism; Horrorism; Dystopianism; Disasterism

 Realism; Italian Neo-Realism; Westernism; Dogmetism; Minimalism

REFERENCE
SECTION

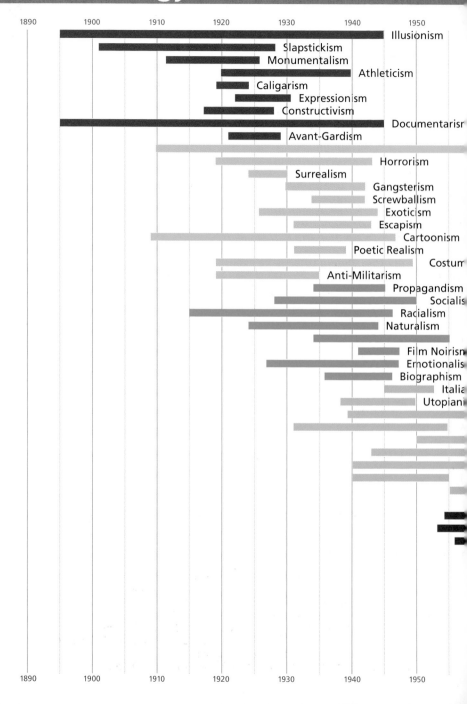

1890　1900　1910　1920　1930　1940　1950

Illusionism
Slapstickism
Monumentalism
Athleticism
Caligarism
Expressionism
Constructivism
Documentarism
Avant-Gardism
Horrorism
Surrealism
Gangsterism
Screwballism
Exoticism
Escapism
Cartoonism
Poetic Realism
Costum
Anti-Militarism
Propagandism
Socialis
Racialism
Naturalism
Film Noirism
Emotionalis
Biographism
Italia
Utopian

1890　1900　1910　1920　1930　1940　1950

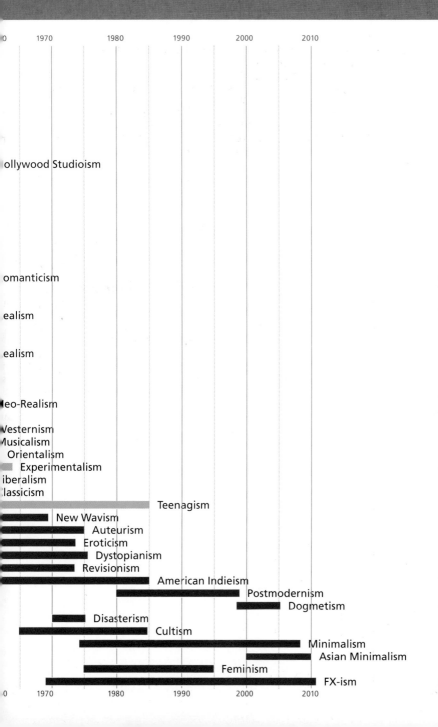

CINEMA NUOVO

The 'new cinema' that flourished in Brazil in the 1960s, and sought to establish a political cinema with a revolutionary spirit.

CINÉMA VERITÉ

Literally 'truthful cinema', this applies to a series of documentary films which strive for immediacy, spontaneity and authenticity. The term was first used in reference to Jean Rouch's *Chronicle of a Summer* (1960).
see *Kino-Pravda*

COMPUTER-GENERATED IMAGERY (CGI)

Images brought about through digital computer technology, first introduced in the 1970s.

CRANE SHOT

A shot taken from a camera mounted on a crane that can vary distance, height and angles. High overhead shots were a speciality of dance director Busby Berkeley.

CROSS-CUTTING

An editing technique that cuts back and forth between actions in separate spaces implying simultaneity. This was first used most effectively by DW Griffith and Abel Gance.
see *Dynamic Cutting and Montage*

DEEP FOCUS

When multiple planes in the shot – objects or characters in the foreground, middle ground and background – are all brought into sharp focus simultaneously. This was brought about by a wide-angle lens developed in the 1930s.

DEPTH OF FIELD

The range and distance between the main focus of the shot within which objects remain sharp and clear.

DIEGESIS

A term that refers to the film's story, characters, places and events, the internal world created by the story that the characters themselves experience and encounter.

DIEGETIC

Includes all music and dialogue in normal space and time that is part of the action of the film, and has its source in the narrative which the characters can see and hear. Voice-over and music on the sound track is non-diegetic. For example, if a character in the film is playing music it is diegetic sound. On the other hand, the accompanying music on the soundtrack, not heard by the characters, is non-diegetic.

DIRECT SOUND

Sound captured directly from its source without dubbing or sound effects.

DISSOLVE

A transition between two scenes whereby the first gradually fades out and the second gradually fades in with some overlap between the two. Rapid dissolves suggest an immediate dramatic contrast while slow dissolves suggest a more gradual passing of time.

DOLLY

A platform on wheels mounted with a movie camera.

DOLLY SHOT

A shot in which the camera moves towards the subject (to dolly in) or back from it (to dolly out).
see *Tracking Shot*

DYNAMIC CUTTING

Editing a series of abrupt shots of people and objects not necessarily from the same scene, thus breaking the sense of continuous action but all functioning together. The individual shots function in juxtaposition to one another creating a synthesis of a single context to create tension and emotions in the audience. This is used to devastating effect in Sergei Eisenstein's films of the 1920s.
see *Cross-Cutting and Montage*

EMPTY SHOT

When the camera stays on a scene before the entrance or after the exit of characters.

ESTABLISHING SHOT

A shot at the beginning of a sequence, establishing location, mood or information. Re-establishing shots may continue throughout the film to remind the audience of location or to suggest the passage of time.

HAYS CODE

Derived from the name of Will H Hays, the president of the Motion Pictures and Producers and Distributors of America (MPPDA), a studio-generated self-governing system to ensure acceptable levels of moral behaviour.
see *Production Code*

INTERTITLES

Also known as title cards. Printed texts in the midst of the action of a silent film to convey dialogue or to explain location or narrative points not covered by what is seen.

JUMP CUT

A cut between two shots that seems abrupt, moving rapidly in time and space. Long thought to be the result of bad direction and editing, it was first used creatively in Jean-Luc Godard's *Breathless* (1960).

KINO-PRAVDA

A series of newsreels and documentaries recording everyday eventsmade by Djiga Vertov (Denis Kaufman) in the early days of the Russian Revolution
see *Cinéma Verité*

LONG SHOT
A shot that shows the subject at a distance. Characters are seen in their entirety usually in relationship to their environment.

LONG TAKE
A shot or take that lasts for a longer time than is usual without relying on cutting from shot to shot. Most famous examples are Alfred Hitchcock's *Rope* (1948), which is a series of 10-minute takes (the limit for each reel) and Aleksandr Sokurov's *Russian Ark* (2002), a 96-minute film consisting of a single take.

MEDIUM SHOT
Between long shot and close-up, it shows a character from the waist up or seated. Effective in showing two characters or as a transitional shot.

MISE-EN-SCÈNE
Literally 'put on stage', it refers to the composition and placement within an individual frame rather than to the acting or editing.

MONTAGE
A juxtaposition of opposing cinematic images.
see *Dynamic Cutting and Cross-Cutting*

PAINTED CELS
The individual components of traditional animation whereby figures are drawn and painted on transparent cellulose acetate (originally on celluloid hence cell) sheets.

PAN
A compression of 'panorama' or 'panoramic', it is a horizontal movement of the camera on a fixed plane.
see *Tracking Shot and Dolly Shot*

PIXILATION
A type of animation, achieved by a stop-frame camera, and perfected by the Canadian animator Norman Mclaren which uses people or objects to create speeded up, jerky movements for a cartoon effect.
see *Stop Motion*

POINT-OF-VIEW SHOT (POV)
A subjective shot that reproduces what a character sees often preceded by shots of the character looking. Robert Montgomery's *The Lady in the Lake* (1946) is the only mainstream feature which uses POV throughout, the whole story being seen through the hero's eyes.

PRODUCTION CODE
Set up in 1922 by the film industry in response to public indignation over apparent sex scandals in Hollywood, it applied pressure on the studios to control the moral content of films. The Code was finally replaced by a movie ratings system in 1968.
see *Hays Code*

SHOT REVERSE SHOT
Probably the most common technique of cutting which begins with a close-up of a character taken from an angle followed by another close-up of a second character taken from a reverse angle, continuing back and forth through the sequence.
see *Two Shot*

STOP MOTION
A technique that uses the stopping and starting of a camera, often a single frame at a time, which is then synthesised on film to produce the effect of movement.
see *Pixilation*

SUPERIMPOSITION
The simultaneous appearance of two or more images over one another in the same frame. Among the most celebrated uses are in Sergei Eisenstein's *The Strike* (1924), when heads of animals are superimposed on those of men, and the last scene of Alfred Hitchcock's *Psycho* (1960) when, for a split second, the skull of the mother is superimposed on the face of Norman Bates.

THREE-STRIP TECHNICOLOR
Colour processing, developed in 1932, in which three strips of film – red, blue and green – are transferred onto a single image.
see *Two-Strip Technicolor*

TRACKING SHOT
A shot created by a camera mounted on a dolly or track which follows the movement of an actor or action in any direction – forward, backwards, behind or around the subject.
see *Dolly Shot*

TWO SHOT
A medium shot in which two people fill the frame, often created by the classical shot reverse shot.
see *Shot Reverse Shot*

TWO-STRIP TECHNICOLOR
A film colour process, patented in 1922, originally with only two colours – red and green. Chester M Franklin's *Toll of the Sea* (1922) was the first Technicolor feature film able to be projected through a normal film projector, and therefore was the first to be given a release.
see *Three-Strip Technicolor*

A

ABRAHAMS, Jim 1944–; Disasterism

ADAMSON, Andrew 1966–; Cartoonism

AKERMAN, Chantal 1950–; Feminism

ALEXANDROV, Grigori 1903–83; Escapism; Musicalism

ALGAR, James: 1912–98; Cartoonism

ALLEN, Irwin 1916–91; Disasterism

ALLEN, Woody 1935–; Escapism; Postmodernism

ALMODÓVAR, Pedro 1949–; Emotionalism; Eroticism; Feminism; Revisionism

ALDRICH, Robert 1918–83; Film Noirism

ALTMAN, Robert 1925–2006; Revisionism

D'AMICO, Suso Cecchi 1914–; Italian Neo-Realism

ANDERSON, Lindsay 1923–94; Naturalism

ANDERSON, Michael 1920–; Dystopianism

ANDERSSON, Roy 1943–; Surrealism

ANGELOPOULOS, Theo 1935–; Liberalism; Minimalism

ANGER, Kenneth 1927–; Experimentalism; Surrealism

ANTONIONI, Michelangelo 1912–2007; Auteurism

ARBUCKLE, Roscoe 'Fatty' 1887–1933; Slapstickism

ARGENTO, Dario 1940–; Horrorism

ARLISS, Leslie 1901–87; Costume Romanticism

ASHER, William 1921–; Teenagism

ATTENBOROUGH, Richard 1923–; Anti-Militarism; Biographism

AUTANT-LARA, Claude 1901–2000; Classicism

AVERY, Tex 1908–80; Cartoonism

B

BACON, Lloyd 1889–1955; Hollywood Studioism; Musicalism

BADHAM, John 1939–; Musicalism

BARBERA, Joe 1911–2006; Cartoonism

BARNET, Boris 1902–1965; Constructivism

BARR, Jean-Marc 1960–; Dogmetism

BAVA, Mario 1914–80; Horrorism

BAY, Michael 1965–; Disasterism

BEINEX, Jean-Jacques 1946–; Postmodernism

BELMONDO, Jean-Paul 1933–; Athleticism

BENNING, James 1942–; Experimentalism

BERGMAN, Ingmar 1918–2007; Auteurism; Eroticism; Expressionism; Feminism

BERKELEY, Busby 1895–1976; Illusionism; Musicalism

BERRI, Claude 1934–2009; Naturalism

BERTOLUCCI, Bernardo 1940–; Biographism; Costume Romanticism; Eroticism

BESSON, Luc 1959–; Postmodernism

BIER, Susanne 1960–; Dogmetism

BOESE, Carl 1887–1958; Caligarism; Horrorism

BOETTICHER, Budd 1916–2001; Westernism

BOGART, Humphrey 1899–1957; Gangsterism

BOGDANOVICH, Peter 1939–; Screwballism

BONDARCHUK, Sergei 1920–94; Anti-Militarism

BOROWCZYK, Walerian 1923–2006; Surrealism

BORZAGE, Frank 1893–1962; Emotionalism

BRAKHAGE, Stan 1933–2003; Experimentalism

BRESSON, Robert 1907–99; Auteurism; Minimalism

BRICKMAN, Paul 1949–; Teenagism

DE BROCA, Philippe 1933–2004; Athleticism

BROOKS, Richard 1912–92; Teenagism

BROWN, Clarence 1890–1987; Costume Romanticism; FX-ism

BROWNING, Tod 1880–1962; Expressionism; Hollywood Studioism; Horrorism

BRUCKMAN, Clyde 1894–1955; Slapstickism

BUCQUET, Harold S 1891–1946; Racialism

BUÑUEL, Luis 1900–83; Auteurism; Eroticism; Surrealism

BURTON, Tim 1958–; Caligarism; Expressionism; FX-ism; Illusionism

C

CAGNEY, James 1899–1986; Gangsterism

CAMERON, James 1954–; Disasterism; Dystopianism; FX-ism

CAMPION, Jane 1954–; Feminism

CAPRA, Frank 1897–1991; Hollywood Studioism; Screwballism; Utopianism

CARAX, Leos 1960–; Postmodernism

CARNÉ, Marcel 1909–96; Classicism; Naturalism; Poetic Realism

CASERINI, Mario 1874–1920; Disasterism; Monumentalism

CASSAVETES, John 1929–89; American Indieism; Naturalism

LA CAVA, Gregory 1892–1952; Screwballlism

CHABROL, Claude 1930–; New Wavism

CHAN, Jackie 1954–; Athleticism

CHAPLIN, Charlie 1889–1977; Slapstickism

CHARELL, Erik 1885–1974; Escapism; Musicalism

CHEN, Kaige 1952–; Orientalism

CHENAL, Pierre 1904–90; Poetic Realism

CHÉREAU, Patrice 1944–; Costume Romanticism

CHYTILOVA, Vera 1929–; New Wavism

CHOMET, Sylvain 1963–; Cartoonism

CHOW, Stephen 1962–; Athleticism

CLAIR, René 1898–1981; Escapism; Musicalism; Surrealism

CLARK, Bob 1939–2007; Teenagism

CLOUSE, Robert 1928–97; Athleticism

CLOUZOT, Henri-Georges 1907–77; Film Noirism; Horrorism

COCTEAU, Jean 1889–1963; Illusionism; Surrealism

COEN, Ethan 1957–; American Indieism; Postmodernism; Revisionism

COEN, Joel 1954–; American Indieism; Postmodernism; Revisionism

COHN, Harry 1891–1958; Hollywood Studioism

COLBERT, Claudette 1903–96; Screwballism

CONNER, Bruce 1933–2008; Experimentalism

CONWAY, Jack 1887–1952; Racialism

COOPER, Merian C 1893–1973; Disasterism; Documentarism

COPPOLA, Francis Ford 1939–; Anti-Militarism; Gangsterism; Teenagism

CORMAN, Roger 1926–; American Indieism; Horrorism; Surrealism

COSTA-GAVRAS 1933–; Liberalism

COSTNER, Kevin 1955–; Westernism

CRAWFORD, Joan 1904–77; Emotionalism

CRONENBERG, David 1943–; FX-ism; Postmodernism

CROSLAND, Alan 1894–1936; Racialism

CUARÓN, Alfonso 1961–; Eroticism

CUKOR, George 1899–1983; Classicism; Screwballism

CURTIZ, Michael 1888–1962; Biographism; Classicism; Emotionalism; Gangsterism; Hollywood Studioism

D

DARDENNE, Jean-Pierre 1951–; Realism

DARDENNE, Luc 1954–; Realism

DAVIS, Bette 1908–89; Emotionalism

DELLUC, Louis 1890–1924; Avant-Gardism

DEMILLE, Cecille B 1881–1959; FX-ism; Monumentalism; Racialism; Utopianism

DEMY, Jacques 1931–90; Escapism; Musicalism

DEPARDON, Raymond 1942–; Documentarism

DEREN, Maya 1917–61; Experimentalism

DIETERLE, William 1893–1972; Biographism

DISNEY, Walt 1901–66; Cartoonism; Racialism

DMYTRYK, Edward 1908–99; Film Noirism; Liberalism

DONEN, Stanley 1924–; Hollywood Studioism; Musicalism

DONSKOI, Mark 1901–81; Socialist Realism

DOUGLAS, Gordon 1907–93; Propagandism

DOVZHENKO, Alexander 1894–1956; Propagandism; Socialist Realism

DREYER, Carl 1889–1968; Auteurism; Feminism; Horrorism

DUDOW, Slatan 1903–63; Propagandism

DULAC, Germaine 1882–1942; Feminism; Surrealism

DUPONT, EA 1891–1956; Expressionism

DURAS, Marguerite 1914–96; Feminism

DUVIVIER, Julien 1896–1967; Poetic Realism

DWAN, Allan 1885–1981; Athleticism

E

EASTWOOD, Clint 1930–; Anti-Militarism; Revisionism; Westernism

EISENSTEIN, Sergei 1898–1948; Constructivism; Costume Romanticism; Propagandism; Socialist Realism

EMMERICH, Roland 1955–; Disasterism

EPSTEIN, Jean 1897–1953; Avant-Gardism

F

FAIRBANKS, Douglas 1883–1939; Athleticism

FASSBINDER, Rainer Werner 1946–82; Emotionalism; Feminism; Minimalism; Revisionism

FELLINI, Federico 1920–93; Auteurism; Italian Neo-Realism

FEYDER, Jacques 1887–1948; Feminism; Poetic Realism

FISCHINGER, Oskar 1900–67; Avant-Gardism

FLAHERTY, Robert 1884–1951; Documentarism; Exoticism

FLEISCHER, Richard 1916–2006; Dystopianism

FLEISHER, Dave 1894–1979; Cartoonism

FLEISHER, Max 1883–1972; Cartoonism

FLEMING, Victor 1889–1949; Classicism; Costume Romanticism; Escapism; Illusionism; Racialism; Utopianism

FLYNN, Errol 1909–59; Athleticism

FOLMAN, Ari 1962–; Cartoonism

FORD, John 1894–1973; Anti-Militarism; Auteurism; Biographism; Classicism; Disasterism; Exoticism; Liberalism; Racialism; Utopianism; Westernism

FORMAN, Miloš 1932–; Biographism; New Wavism

FOSSE, Bob 1927–87; Musicalism

FRAMPTON, Hollis 1936–84; Experimentalism

FREARS, Stephen 1941–; Costume Romanticism

FREED, Arthur 1894–1973; Musicalism

FREUND, Karl 1890–1969; Expressionism; Horrorism

FRIEDKIN, William 1935–; Horrorism

FUKASAKU, Kinji 1930–2003; Teenagism

FULLER, Sam 1912–97; Anti-Militarism

FULTON, John P 1902–66; FX-ism

G

GABIN, Jean 1904–76; Poetic Realism

GALLONE, Carmine 1886–1973; Disasterism

GANCE, Abel 1889–1981; Anti-Militarism; Biographism

GARNETT, Tay 1894–1977; Exoticism

GASNIER, Louis J 1875–1963; Cultism

GILLIAM, Terry 1940–; Dystopianism; Illusionism

GODARD, Jean-Luc 1930–; Auteurism; Dystopianism; Film Noirism; New Wavism; Revisionism

GOULDING, Edmund 1891–1959; Emotionalism; Hollywood Studioism

GRANT, Cary 1904–86; Screwballism

GREEN, Alfred E 1889–1960; Biographism

GREENAWAY, Peter 1942–; Avant-Gardism; Costume Romanticism

GRÉMILLON, Jean 1901–59; Naturalism

GRIERSON, John 1898–1972; Documentarism; Propagandism

GRIFFITH, DW 1875–1948; Disasterism; Emotionalism; Monumentalism; Propagandism; Racialism

GUEST, Val 1911–2006; Disasterism

GUILLERMIN, John 1925–; Disasterism

GUY, Alice 1873–1968; Feminism

H

HACKFORD, Taylor 1944–; Biographism

HAMMID, Alexander 1907–2004; Experimentalism

HANNA, William 1910–2001; Cartoonism

HANSON, Curtis 1945–; Revisionism

HARA, Kazuo 1945–; Documentarism

HARDY, Oliver 1892–1957; Slapstickism

HARDY, Robin 1939–; Cultism

HARLAN, Veit 1899–1964; Propagandism; Racialism

HARRYHAUSEN, Ray 1920–; FX-ism

HARTLEY, Hal 1959–; American Indieism

HAS, Wojciech 1925–2000; Illusionism; Surrealism

HAWKS, Howard 1896–1977; Anti-Militarism; Classicism; Feminism; Film Noirism; Gangsterism; Monumentalism; Screwballism; Westernism

HAYNES, Todd 1961–; Emotionalism

HEIFITS, Josef 1905–95; Socialist Realism

HELLMAN, Monte 1932–; Cultism

HEPBURN, Katharine 1907–2003; Screwballism

L'HERBIER, Marcel 1890–1979; Avant-Gardism

HERZOG, Werner 1942–; Auteurism; Cultism; Exoticism

HIPPLER, Fritz 1909–2002; Racialism

HITCHCOCK, Alfred 1899–1980; Auteurism; Expressionism; FX-ism; Horrorism; Utopianism

HONDA, Ishirô 1911–93; Disasterism; FX-ism

HOPPER, Dennis 1935–2010; American Indieism

HORNE, James W 1880–1942; Athleticism

HSIAO-HSIEN, Hou 1947–; Asian Minimalism

HUGHES, John 1950–2009; Teenagism

HUILLET, Danièle 1936–2006; Avant-Gardism; Minimalism

HUNG TRAN, Anh 1962–; Asian Minimalism

HUNTER, Ross 1920–96; Escapism

HUSTON, John 1906–87; Film Noirism

I

ICHIKAWA, Kon 1915–2008; Anti-Militarism

IMAMURA, Shohei 1926–2006; Orientalism

ISOU, Isidore 1925–2007; Experimentalism

IVORY, James 1928–; Costume Romanticism

J

JACKSON, Peter 1961–; Disasterism; FX-ism

JANCSÓ, Miklós 1921–; Auteurism

JARMUSCH, Jim 1953–; American Indieism; Minimalism; Revisionism

JENNINGS, Humphrey 1907–50; Propagandism

JEWISON, Norman 1926–; Liberalism

JODOROWSKY, Alejandro 1929–; Cultism

JONES, Chuck 1912–2002; Cartoonism

JONZE, Spike 1969– ; Surrealism

JOST, Jon 1943–; Experimentalism

JULIAN, Rupert 1879–1943; Horrorism

K

KANIN, Garson 1912–99; Screwballism

KAR-WAI, Wong 1958–; Orientalism; Revisionism

KAUFMAN, Charlie 1958–; Surrealism

KAURISMÄKI, Aki 1957–; Minimalism

KAZAN, Elia 1909–2003; Classicism; Eroticism; Liberalism; Teenagism

KEATON, Buster 1895–1966; Athleticism; Slapstickism

KELLY, Gene 1912–96; Hollywood Studioism; Musicalism

KIAROSTAMI, Abbas 1940–; Feminism; Minimalism; Realism

KI-DUK, Kim 1960–; Orientalism

KIESLOWSKI, Krzysztof 1941–96; Auteurism

KING, Henry 1888–1982; Disasterism; Utopianism; Westernism

KITANO, Takeshi 1947–; Gangsterism

KLEISER, Randal 1946– ; Musicalism; Teenagism

KLIMOV, Elem 1933–2003; Anti-Militarism

KOBAYASHI, Masaki 1916–96; Horrorism

KORDA, Alexander 1893–1956; Costume Romanticism

KORDA, Zoltan 1895–1961; Exoticism

KORE-EDA, Hirokazu 1962–; Asian Minimalism

KORINE, Harmony 1973–; Dogmetism

KOSTER, Henry 1905–88; Monumentalism

KOZINTSEV, Grigori 1905–73; Constructivism; Socialist Realism

KRAGH-JACOBSEN, Søren 1947–; Dogmetism

KRAMER, Stanley 1913–2001; Liberalism; Slapstickism

KUBRICK, Stanley 1928–99; Anti-Militarism; Costume Romanticism; FX-ism; Liberalism

KUCHAR, George 1942–; Experimentalism

KULESHOV, Lev 1899–1970; Constructivism

KUROSAWA, Akira 1912–98; Auteurism; Gangsterism; Orientalism

KUROSAWA, Kiyoshi 1955–; Horrorism

KWON-TAEK, Im 1936–; Orientalism

L

LAEMMLE, Carl 1867–1939; Hollywood Studioism

LANCASTER, Burt 1913–94; Athleticism

LANDIS, John 1950–; Teenagism

LANG, Fritz 1890–1976; Caligarism; Dystopianism; Expressionism; Film Noirism; FX-ism; Naturalism

LANGDON, Harry 1894–1944; Slapstickism

LANZMANN, Claude 1925–; Documentarism

LASSETER, John 1957–; Cartoonism

LAUREL, Stan 1890–1965; Slapstickism

LEACOCK, Richard 1921–; Documentarism

LEAN, David 1908–91; Biographism; Classicism; Costume Romanticism

LEE, Ang 1954–; Athleticism; Orientalism

LEE, Bruce 1940–73; Athleticism

LEE, Spike 1957–; American Indieism; Biographism

LEGER, Fernand 1881–1955; Avant-Gardism

LEIGH, Mike 1943–; Naturalism; Realism

LEISEN, Mitchell 1897–1972; Screwballism

LENI, Paul 1885–1929; Caligarism; Horrorism

LEONE, Sergio 1929–89; Revisionism; Westernism

LEROY, Mervyn 1900–87; Gangsterism: Hollywood Studioism; Monumentalism

LESTER, Richard 1932–; Teenagism

LEVRING, Kristian 1957–; Dogmetism

LEWTON, Val 1904–51; Horrorism

LIPSKÝ, Oldrich 1924–86; Revisionism

LINDER, Max 1883–1925; Slapstickism

LLOYD, Harold 1893–1971; Slapstickism

LOACH, Ken 1936–; Realism

LOMBARD, Carole 1908–42; Screwballism

LORENTZ, Pare 1905–92; Propagandism

LUBITSCH, Ernst 1892–1947; Classicism; Costume Romanticism; Eroticism; Escapism; Hollywood Studioism; Musicalism

LUCAS, George 1944–; FX-ism; Teenagism

LUHRMANN, Baz 1962–; Musicalism

LUMET, Sidney 1924–; Liberalism

LYNCH, David 1946–; American Indieism; Postmodernism; Surrealism

M

MACH, Josef 1909–87; Revisionism

MADDIN, Guy 1956–; Postmodernism

MAKHMALBAF, Samira 1977–; Feminism

MALLE, Louis 1932–95; Eroticism; New Wavism

MAMOULIAN, Rouben 1897–1987; Costume Romanticism; Musicalism

MANKIEWICZ, Joseph L 1909–93; Classicism; Monumentalism

MANN, Anthony 1906–67; Monumentalism; Westernism

MARAIS, Jean 1913–98; Athleticism

MARKER, Chris 1921–; Avant-Gardism; Documentarism; Dystopianism

MARKOPOULOS, Gregory 1928–92; Experimentalism

MAYER, Louis B 1884–1957; Hollywood Studioism

MAYSLES, Albert 1926–; Documentarism

MAYSLES, David 1931–87; Documentarism

MCCAREY, Leo 1898–1969; Escapism; Screwballism; Surrealism

MCCAY, Winsor 1871–1934; Cartoonism

MCLAREN, Norman 1914–87; Cartoonism

MEKAS, Jonas 1922–; Experimentalism

MÉLIÈS, Georges 1861–1938; Biographism; FX-ism; Horrorism

MELVILLE, Jean-Pierre 1917–73; Gangsterism

MENZIES, William Cameron 1896–1957; Dystopianism

MESHKINI, Marzieh 1969–; Feminism

MEYER, Russ 1922–2004; Cultism

MIFUNE, Toshiro 1920–97; Athleticism

MIIKE, Takashi 1960–; Horrorism

MILESTONE, Lewis 1895–1980; Anti-Militarism

MILLER, George 1945–; Dystopianism

MING-LIANG, Tsai 1957–; Asian Minimalism

MINNELLI, Vincente 1903–86; Biographism; Classicism; Musicalism; Utopianism

MIYAZAKI, Hayao 1941–; Cartoonism

MIZOGUCHI, Kenji 1898–1956; Auteurism; Orientalism

MONTGOMERY, Robert 1904–81; Film Noirism

MOORE, Michael 1954–; Documetarism; Liberalism

MORRIS, Errol 1948–; Documentarism

MULLIGAN, Robert 1925–2008; Liberalism

MUNGIU, Cristian 1968–; Minimalism

MUNI, Paul 1895–1967); Biographism

MURNAU, FW 1889–1931; Caligarism; Exoticism; Expressionism; FX-ism

N

NAKATA, Hideo 1961–; Horrorism

NEAME, Ronald 1911–; Disasterism

NEGULESCO, Jean 1900–93; Escapism; Hollywood Studioism

NEWMEYER, Fred C 1881–1967; Slapstickism

NIBLO, Fred 1874–1948; Athleticism; Monumentalism

O

O'BRIEN, Willis 1886–1962; FX-ism

OPHÜLS, Marcel 1927–; Documentarism

OPHÜLS, Max 1902–57; Auteurism; Classicism; Costume Romanticism

ÔSHIMA, Nagisa 1932–; Eroticism; New Wavism; Orientalism

OZU, Yasujiro 1903–63; Asian Minimalism; Orientalism

P

PABST, GW 1885–1967; Anti-Militarism; Eroticism; Expressionism; Propagandism

PANAHI, Jafar 1960–; Feminism; Realism

PARAJANOV, Sergei 1924–90; Utopianism

PARK, Chan-Wook 1963–; Orientalism

PARK, Nick 1958–; Cartoonism

PARONNAUD, Vincent 1970–; Cartoonism

PARROTT, James 1897–1939; Slapstickism

PASOLINI, Pier Paolo 1922–75; Auteurism; Italian Neo-Realism

PASTRONE, Giovanni 1883–1959; Monumentalism

PECKINPAH, Sam 1925–84; Revisionism; Westernism

PENN, Arthur 1922–; Gangsterism; Revisionism; Westernism

PETERSEN, Wolfgang 1941–; Anti-Militarism; Disasterism

PHILIBERT, Nicolas 1951–; Documentarism

PIALAT, Maurice 1925–2003; Realism

PICHEL, Irving 1891–1954; Biographism

POLANSKI, Roman 1933–; Eroticism; Film Noirism; Horrorism; Revisionism

PONTECORVO, Gillo 1919–2006; Realism

POWELL, Michael 1905–90; Propagandism; Utopianism

PREMINGER, Otto 1905–86; Classicism; Film Noirism

PRESSBURGER, Emeric 1902–88; FX-ism; Propagandism; Utopianism

PRÉVERT, Jacques 1900–77; Poetic Realism

PROTAZANOV, Yakov 1881–1945; Constructivism; Utopianism

PUDOVKIN, Vsevolod 1893–1953; Socialist Realism

PUIU, Cristi 1967–; Minimalism

R

RADFORD, Michael 1946–; Dystopianism

RAFT, George 1895–1980; Gangsterism

RAPPER, Irving 1898–1999;
Emotionalism

RAY, Man 1890–1976; Avant-Gardism;
Surrealism

RAY, Nicholas 1911–79; Biographism;
Monumentalism; Teenagism

RAY, Satyajit 1921–92; Feminism;
Realism

REINER, Carl 1922–; Film Noirism

REINER, Rob 1947–; Cultism

REINIGER, Lotte 1899–1981;
Cartoonism

REISNER, Charles 1887–1962;
Slapstickism

RENOIR, John 1894–1979; Anti-
Militarism; Naturalism; Poetic Realism;
Realism

RESNAIS, Alain 1922–;
Documentarism; Naturalism; New
Wavism; Surrealism

REYGADAS, Carlos 1971–; Minimalism

RICHTER, Hans 1888–1976; Avant-
Gardism

RIEFENSTAHL, Leni 1902–2003;
Propagandism

RITT, Martin 1914–90; Liberalism

RIVETTE, Jacques 1928–; New Wavism

ROACH, Hal 1892–1992; Slapstickism

ROBBINS, Jerome 1918–98; Musicalism

ROBINSON, Bruce 1946–; Cultism

ROBINSON, Edward G 1893–1973;
Gangsterism

ROBSON, Mark 1913–78; Disasterism

ROCHA, Glauber 1938–81; New
Wavism

RODOLFI, Eleuterio 1876–1933;
Disasterism

ROHMER, Éric 1920–2010; New
Wavism

ROMERO, George 1940–; American
Indieism; Horrorism

ROMM, Mikhail 1901–77; Biographism

ROSSELLINI, Roberto 1906–77;
Costume Romanticism; Italian Neo-
Realism

ROUCH, Jean 1917–2004;
Documentarism

RUSSELL, Ken 1927–; Biographism

RUTTMANN, Walter 1887–1941;
Avant-Gardism

S

SANDRICH, Mark 1900–45;
Hollywood Studioism

SANG SOO, Hong 1960–; Asian
Minimalism

SANTIS, Giuseppe De 1917–77; Italian
Neo-Realism

SATRAPI, Marjane 1969–; Cartoonism

SAURA, Carlos 1932–; Liberalism

SCHAFFNER, Franklin J 1920–89;
Biographism

SCHERFIG, Lone 1959–; Dogmetism

SCHOEDSACK, Ernest 1893–1979;
Disasterism; Documentarism

SCORSESE, Martin 1942–; Athleticism;
Biographism; Classicism; Costume
Romanticism

SCOTT, Randolph 1898–1987;
Westernism

SCOTT, Ridley 1937–; Dystopianism;
Expressionism; Feminism; Film Noirism;
Monumentalism; Postmodernism

SEATON, George 1911–79; Disasterism

SENNETT, Mack 1880–1960;
Slapstickism

SHARMAN, Jim 1945– ; Cultism

DE SICA, Vittorio 1902–74; Italian
Neo-Realism

SIDNEY, George 1916–2002;
Musicalism

SIODMAK, Robert 1900–73;
Athleticism; Exoticism; Film Noirism

SIRK, Douglas 1897–1987; Classicism;
Emotionalism

SMITH, Kevin 1970–; American
Indieism

SNOW, Michael 1929–;
Experimentalism

SODERBERGH, Steven 1963–;
American Indieism

SOLNTSEVA, Yuliya 1901–89; Socialist
Realism

SPIELBERG, Steven 1946–; Escapism;
FX-ism

STAHL, John 1886–1950; Emotionalism

STANWYCK, Barbara 1907–90;
Emotionalism

STEVENS, George 1904–75;
Westernism

STONE, Oliver 1946–; Liberalism

STRAUB, Jean-Marie 1933–; Avant-
Gardism; Minimalism

STURGES, John 1910–92; Westernism

STURGES, Preston 1898–1959;
Screwballism

SULLAVAN, Margaret 1909–60;
Emotionalism

SULLIVAN, Pat 1887–1933; Cartoonism

ŠVANKMAJER, Jan 1934–; Illusionism;
Surrealism

T

TARANTINO, Quentin 1963–;
American Indieism; Gangsterism;
Postmodernism

TARKOVSKY, Andrei 1932–86;
Auteurism

TARR, Béla 1955–; Minimalism

TAYLOR, Sam 1895–1958; Slapstickism

THALBERG, Irving 1899–1936;
Hollywood Studioism

THORPE, Richard 1896–1991;
Monumentalism

TO, Johnnie 1955–; Gangsterism

TOURNEUR, Jacques 1904–77;
Athleticism; Film Noirism; Horrorism

TRAUBERG, Leonid 1902–90;
Constructivism; Socialist Realism

TRAUNER, Alexandre 1906–93; Poetic
Realism

TRNKA, Jirí 1912–69; Cartoonism

TRUFFAUT, François 1932–84;
Dystopianism; New Wavism; Revisionism

TRUMBULL, Douglas 1942–; FX-ism

TYKWER, Tom 1965–; Postmodernism

V

VADIM, Roger 1928–2000; Eroticism

VAN DYKE, WS 1889–1943;
Disasterism

VAN SANT, Gus 1952–; American
Indieism; Biographism; Dogmetism

VARDA, Agnès 1928–; Feminism; New
Wavism

VASILYEV, Georgi 1899–1946; Socialist
Realism

VASILYEV, Sergei 1900–59; Socialist
Realism

VERTOV, Dziga 1896–1954;
Constructivism

VIDOR, Charles 1900–59; Biographism

VIDOR, King 1894–1982; Emotionalism

VIGO, Jean 1905–34; Realism

VINTERBERG, Thomas 1969–;
Dogmetism

VISCONTI, Luchino 1906–76; Costume
Romanticism; Italian Neo-Realism;
Naturalism

VON BÁKY, Josef 1902–66; Escapism:
Illusionism

VON STERNBERG, Josef 1894–1969;
Eroticism; Exoticism; Expressionism

VON STROHEIM, Eric 1885–1957;
Exoticism; Naturalism

VON TRIER, Lars 1956–; Dogmetism

W

WACHOWSKI, Andy 1967–;
Dystopianism; Postmodernism

WACHOWSKI, Larry 1965–;
Dystopianism; Postmodernism

WADLEIGH, Michael 1942– ;
Teenagism

WAJDA, Andrzej 1926–;
Anti-Militarism; Liberalism

WALSH, Raoul 1887–1980;
Athleticism; Film Noirism; FX-ism;
Gangsterism: Illusionism; Westernism

WALTERS, Charles 1911–82;
Musicalism

WARHOL, Andy 1928–87;
Avant-Gardism; Experimentalism

WARNER, Jack 1892–1978; Hollywood
Studioism

WATERS, John 1946–; Cultism

WAYNE, John 1907–79; Westernism

WEERASETHAKUL , Apichatpong
1970–; Asian Minimalism

WEGENER, Paul 1874–1948;
Caligarism; Horrorism

WEITZ, Chris 1969–; Teenagism

WEITZ, Paul 1965–; Teenagism

WELLES, Orson 1915–85; Film Noirism;
Auteurism

WELLMAN, William 1896–1975;
Gangsterism; Racialism

WHALE, James 1889–1957; Caligarism;
Expressionism; Horrorism

WIENE, Robert 1873–1938; Caligarism

WILDER, Billy 1906–2002; Classicism;
Film Noirism

WISE, Robert 1914–2005; Cultism;
Horrorism; Monumentalism

WISEMAN, Fred 1930–;
Documentarism

WOO, John 1946–; Gangsterism;
Orientalism

WOOD, Ed Jr 1924–78; Cultism

WYLER, William 1902–81; Classicism;
Monumentalism; Westernism

X

XIE, Jin 1923–2008; Socialist Realism

Y

YANG, Edward 1947–2007; Asian
Minimalism

YIMOU, Zhang 1951–; Orientalism

YUTKEVICH, Sergei 1904–85; Socialist
Realism

Z

ZANUCK, Darryl F 1902–79;
Hollywood Studioism

ZARKHI, Alexander 1908–97; Socialist
Realism

ZAVATTINI, Cesare 1902–89; Italian
Neo-Realism

ZEMAN, Karel 1910–89; Cartoonism

ZEMECKIS, Robert 1952–; Escapism;
FX-ism

ZHANG KE, Jia 1970–; Asian
Minimalism

ZINNEMANN, Fred 1907–97;
Eroticism; Westernism

ZUCKER, David 1947–; Disasterism

ZUCKER, Jerry 1950– ; Disasterism

ZUKOR, Adolph 1873–1976;
Hollywood Studioism

A

Accatone, 1961; Italian Neo-Realism

The Adventures of Robin Hood, 1938; Athleticism

Aerograd, 1935; Socialist Realism

L'âge d'or (The Golden Age), 1930; Surrealism

The Age of Innocence, 1993; Costume Romanticism

Aguirre: The Wrath of God, 1972; Cultism; Exoticism

Airport, 1970; Disasterism

Alexander Nevsky, 1938; Socialist Realism

Alice, 1988; Illusionism

All About Eve, 1950; Classicism

All About My Mother, 1999; Emotionalism; Revisionism

All Quiet on the Western Front, 1930; Anti-Militarism

All That Heaven Allows, 1955; Emotionalism

All That Jazz, (1979); Musicalism

Alphaville, 1965; Dystopianism; Film Noirism; Revisionism

Amadeus, 1984; Biographism

American Graffiti, 1973; Teenagism

An American in Paris, 1951; Musicalism

An Angel at My Table, 1990; Feminism

And God Created Woman, 1956; Eroticism

Angels with Dirty Faces, 1938; Gangsterism

Anna Boleyn, 1920; Costume Romanticism

The Apartment, 1960; Classicism

Apocalypse Now, 1979; Anti-Militarism

The Apu Trilogy (Pather Panchali, The Unvanquished, The World of Apu), 1955, 1956, 1959; Realism

L'argent, 1928; Avant-Gardism

Armageddon, 1998; Disasterism

Arsenal, 1929; Propagandism

Ashes and Diamonds, 1958; Anti-Militarism

L'atalante, 1934; Realism

An Autumn Afternoon; 1962; Orientalism

Avatar, 2009; FX-ism

The Aviator, 2004; Biographism

L'avventura, 1960; Auteurism

B

Baby Doll, 1956; Eroticism

Ballet mécanique, 1924; Avant-Gardism

Baltic Deputy, 1937; Socialist Realism

Batman Returns, 1992; Expressionism

The Battle of Algiers, 1966; Realism

Battle Royale, 2001; Teenagism

The Battleship Potemkin, 1925; Constructivism

Beau Geste, 1939; Racialism

Le beau Serge, 1959; New Wavism

Beauty and the Beast (La belle et la bête), 1945; Illusionism

Becky Sharp, 1935; Costume Romanticism

Being John Malkovich, 1999; Surrealism

Belle de jour, 1967; Eroticism

Ben-Hur: A Tale of the Christ, 1925; Monumentalism

Berlin: Symphony of a Great City, 1927; Avant-Gardism

La bête humaine (The Human Beast); 1938; Naturalism; Poetic Realism

Bicycle Thieves, 1948; Italian Neo-Realism

The Big Country, 1958; Westernism

The Big Heat, 1953; Film Noirism

The Big Lebowski, 1998; Postmodernism

The Big Red One, 1980; Anti-Militarism

The Big Sleep, 1946; Film Noirism

The Birth of a Nation, 1915; Racialism

The Bitter Tears of Petra Von Kant, 1972; Revisionism

Blackboard Jungle, 1955; Teenagism

Black Narcissus, 1947; FX-ism

Blade Runner, 1982; Dystopianism; Expressionism; Film Noirism; Postmodernism

The Blood of the Poet, 1930; Surrealism

Blood Simple, 1984; American Indieism; Revisionism

Blue Velvet, 1986; Postmodernism; Surrealism

Bonnie and Clyde, 1967; Gangsterism

Das Boot, 1981; Anti-Militarism

Born on the Fourth of July, 1989; Liberalism

Brazil, 1985; Dystopianism

The Breakfast Club, 1985; Teenagism

Breathless (À bout de souffle), 1960;

New Wavism; Revisionism

Brigadoon, 1954; Utopianism

Bringing Up Baby, 1938; Screwballism

The Burmese Harp, 1956; Anti-Militarism

C

Cabaret, 1972; Musicalism

The Cabinet of Dr Caligari, 1919; Caligarism

Cabiria, 1914; Monumentalism

Carnival in Flanders, 1935; Feminism

Casablanca, 1943; Classicism; Hollywood Studioism

The Cat and the Canary, 1927; Horrorism

Cat People, 1942; Horrorism

The Celebration 1998; Dogmetism

Chapayev, 1934; Socialist Realism

Charulata (The Lonely Wife), 1964; Feminism

La chienne, 1931; Naturalism

Un chien andalou, 1928; Surrealism

China Seas, 1935; Exoticism

Chinatown, 1974; Film Noirism; Revisionism

Chihwaseon, 2002; Orientalism

The Circle, 2000; Feminism

Citizen Kane, 1941; Auteurism

City Lights, 1931; Slapstickism

Cleo From 5 to 7, 1962; New Wavism

Cleopatra; 1963; Monumentalism

Clerks, 1994; American Indieism

Cobra Woman, 1944; Exoticism

The Colour of Pomegranates, 1969; Utopianism

Congress Dances, 1931; Escapism; Musicalism

La coquille et le clergyman (The Seashell and the Clergyman), 1928; Surrealism

Le corbeau (The Raven), 1943; Film Noirism

Crime and Punishment, 1935; Poetic Realism

Crimes and Misdemeanors, 1989; Postmodernism

Crouching Tiger, Hidden Dragon, 2000; Athleticism

D

Dances with Wolves, 1990; Westernism

Dangerous Liaisons, 1988; Costume Romanticism

The Day After Tomorrow, 2004; Disasterism

The Day the Earth Caught Fire, 1961; Disasterism

The Day I Became a Woman, 2000; Feminism

Days of Glory, 1945; Italian Neo-Realism

Dear Wendy, 2005; Dogmetism

The Death of Mr Lazerescu, 2005; Minimalism

The Defiant Ones, 1958; Liberalism

The Deserter, 1933; Socialist Realism

Le diable au corps, 1947; Classicism

Diary of a Country Priest, 1950; Minimalism

The Diary of a Shinjuka Thief, 1968; New Wavism

The Discreet Charm of the Bourgeoisie, 1972; Surrealism

Diva, 1981; Postmodernism

Dog Star Man, 1964, Experimentalism

Dogville, 2003; Dogmetism

La Dolce Vita, 1960; Auteurism

Do The Right Thing, 1989; American Indieism

Double Indemnity, 1944; Film Noirism

Dracula, 1931; Expressionism; Hollywood Studioism; Horrorism

The Draughtsman's Contract, 1982; Costume Romanticism

Dr Mabuse, The Gambler, 1922; Caligarism; Expressionism

Dr Strangelove, 1963; Liberalism

Dr Zhivago, 1966; Classicism

Duck Soup, 1933; Escapism; Surrealism

E

Earthquake, 1974; Disasterism

East of Eden, 1955; Teenagism

Easy Living, 1937; Screwballism

Easy Rider, 1969; American Indieism

Eat Drink Man Woman, 1994; Orientalism

Edward Scissorhands, 1990; Caligarism

El Cid, 1961; Monumentalism

El Dorado, 1921; Avant-Gardism

Elephant Boy, 1936; Exoticism

El Topo, 1970; Cultism

Les enfants du paradis, 1945; Classicism

Enter the Dragon, 1973; Athleticism

Entr'acte, 1924; Surrealism

Eraserhead, 1977; American Indieism; Surrealism

The Eternal Jew, 1940; Racialism

L'étoile de mer (Star Fish), 1928; Surrealism

Étre et avoir, 2002; Documentarism

The Exorcist, 1973; Horrorism

F

The 400 Blows (Les quatre cents coups); 1959; New Wavism

42nd Street, 1933; Hollywood Studioism; Musicalism

49th Parallel , 1941; Propagandism

4 Months, 3 Weeks and 2 Days, 2007; Minimalism

Fahrenheit 451, 1966; Dystopianism

Fahrenheit 9/11, 2004; Documentarism

The Fall of the House of Usher; 1928; Avant-Gardism

The Falls, 1981; Avant-Gardism

Fantasia (1940); Cartoonism

Far From Heaven, 2002; Emotionalism

Faster Pussycat! Kill! Kill!, 1965; Cultism

Faust, 1926; FX-ism

Fear Eats the Soul, 1973; Emotionalism

Une femme est une femme (A Woman is a Woman), 1961; Revisionism

Ferris Bueller's Day Off, 1986; Teenagism

Fires Were Started, 1943; Propagandism

Fitzcarraldo, 1982; Exoticism

Five Dedicated to Ozu, 2003; Minimalism

Flags of Our Fathers, 2006; Anti-Militarism

The Flame and the Arrow, 1950; Athleticism

The Fly, 1986; FX-ism

Frankenstein, 1931; Expressionism; Horrorism

From Here to Eternity, 1953; Eroticism

Fuckland, 2000; Dogmetism

G

Gandhi, 1982; Biographism

The General, 1926; Slapstickism

The General Line, 1928; Propagandism

A Generation, 1954; Anti-Militarism

Gentleman's Agreement, 1947; Liberalism

Germinal; 1993; Naturalism

Gerry, 2002; Dogmetism

Gertrud, 1964; Feminism

Gladiator, 2000; Monumentalism

Glen or Glenda, 1953; Cultism

The Godfather trilogy, 1972, 1974 and 1990; Gangsterism

Godzilla, 1954; Disasterism

The Golem, 1920; Caligarism; Horrorism

Gone with the Wind, 1939; Classicism; Costume Romanticism; Racialism

The Good, the Bad and the Ugly, 1966; Revisionism

Grand Hotel, 1932; Hollywood Studioism

La grande illusion, 1937; Anti-Militarism

Le grand jeu, 1934; Poetic Realism

The Grapes of Wrath, 1940; Liberalism

Grass, 1925; Documentarism

The Great Train Robbery, 1903; Westernism

Greed, 1924; Naturalism

Guess Who's Coming to Dinner?, 1967; Liberalism

Gueule d'amour (Lover Boy), 1937; Naturalism

The Gunfighter, 1950; Westernism

H

Hannah and Her Sisters, 1986; Escapism

A Hard Day's Night, 1964; Teenagism

The Haunting, 1963; Horrorism

Hearts of the World, 1918; Propagandism

Helen of Troy, 1956; Monumentalism

Hero, 2002; Athleticism

High and Low, 1963; Gangsterism

High Noon, 1952; Westernism

Hiroshima mon amour, 1960; New Wavism

His Girl Friday, 1940; Feminism; Screwballism

Holiday, 1938; Screwballism

Hôtel du Nord, 1938; Poetic Realism

How To Marry a Millionaire, 1953; Escapism; Hollywood Studioism

The House on Trubnaya Square, 1928; Constructivism

Hudson's Bay, 1941; Biographism

Human Desire, 1954; Film Noirism; Naturalism

I

The Idiots, 1998; Dogmetism

I Know Where I'm Going, 1945; Utopianism

Independence Day, 1996; Disasterism

Inglourious Basterds, 2009; Postmodernism

L'inhumaine, 1924; Avant-Gardism

Interview, 2000; Dogmetism

In the Heat of the Night, 1967; Liberalism

In the Realm of the Senses (Ai No corrida), 1976; Eroticism

Intolerance, 1916; Disasterism; Monumentalism

It Happened One Night, 1934; Hollywood Studioism; Screwballism

It's a Mad, Mad, Mad, Mad World, 1963; Slapstickism

It's A Wonderful Life, 1946; Utopianism

Ivan the Terrible; Parts I and II), 1944,1946; Costume Romanticism

I Walked with a Zombie, 1943; Horrorism

I Was a Communist for the FBI, 1951; Propagandism

J

J'accuse, 1919; Anti-Militarism

Japón, 2002; Minimalism

Jaws, 1975; FX-ism

The Jazz Singer, 1927; Racialism

Jeanne Dielman, 23 Quai du Commerce, 1080 Bruxelles, 1975; Feminism

Jeanne D'Arc, 1899; Biographism

Jew Suss, 1940; Propagandism; Racialism

The Jolson Story, 1946; Biographism

Judith of Bethulia, 1914; Monumentalism

Jules and Jim, 1961; New Wavism

Jurassic Park, 1993; FX-ism

K

Kameradschaft, 1931; Propagandism

The Killers, 1946; Film Noirism

King Kong, 1933; Disasterism; FX-ism

King Kong, 2005; Disasterism

King-Size Canary; 1947; Cartoonism

Kiss Me Deadly, 1955; Film Noirism

Kung Fu Hustle, 2004; Athleticism

Kwaidan, 1964; Horrorism

L

LA Confidential, 1997; Revisionism

Lady in the Lake, 1947; Film Noirism

Land of the Pharaohs, 1955; Monumentalism

The Last Days of Pompeii, 1913; Disasterism;

The Last Days of Pompeii, 1926; Disasterism; Monumentalism

The Last Emperor, 1987; Biographism; Costume Romanticism

Last Tango in Paris, 1972; Eroticism

Last Year at Marienbad, 1961; Surrealism

Lawrence of Arabia, 1962; Biographism

Leave Her to Heaven; 1945; Emotionalism

Lenin in 1918, 1939; Biographism

The Leopard, 1963; Costume Romanticism

Letters from Iwo Jima, 2006; Anti-Militarism

The Life and Death of Colonel Blimp, 1943; Utopianism

The Life of Emile Zola, 1937; Biographism

The Life of Oharu, 1952; Orientalism

Listen to Britain, 1942; Propagandism

Little Big Man, 1970; Revisionism; Westernism

Little Caesar, 1930; Gangsterism

The Little Foxes, 1941; Classicism

The Little Shop of Horrors, 1960; American Indieism

The Lodger, 1927; Expressionism

Logan's Run, 1976; Dystopianism

Lola Montès, 1955; Costume Romanticism

London Can Take It, 1940; Propagandism

The Long Goodbye, 1973; Revisionism

Lord of the Rings, 2001; FX-ism

Lost Horizon, 1937; Utopianism

Loulou, 1980; Realism

Lovers, 1999; Dogmetism

The Lovers, 1958; Eroticism

Loves of a Blonde, 1965; New Wavism

Lumière d'été (Summer Light), 1943; Naturalism

Lust for Life, 1956; Biographism

M

M, 1931; Caligarism; Expressionism

Madame DuBarry, 1919; Costume Romanticism

Mad Max, 1979; Dystopianism

The Magnificent Seven, 1960; Westernism

Malcolm X, 1992; Biographism

The Maltese Falcon, 1941; Film Noirism

A Man Escaped, 1956; Auteurism

The Man From Laramie, 1955; Westernism

The Man I Love, 1946; Film Noirism

The Man Who Shot Liberty Valance, 1962; Westernism

The Man Who Wasn't There, 2001; Revisionism

Man with a Movie Camera, 1929; Constructivism

The Man Without a Past, 2002; Minimalism

The Mark of Zorro, 1920; Athleticism

The Marriage of Maria Braun, 1978; Feminism

M*A*S*H, 1970; Revisionism

The Masque of the Red Death, 1964; Horrorism

The Matrix Trilogy: The Matrix, 1999, The Matrix Reloaded, 2003 and The Matrix Revolutions, 2003; Dystopianism; Postmodernism

A Matter of Life and Death, 1946; Utopianism

Meet Me in St Louis, 1944; Utopianism

The Melomaniac, 1903; Illusionism

The Merchant of Four Seasons, 1971; Minimalism

The Merry Widow, 1934; Musicalism

Meshes of the Afternoon, 1943; Experimentalism

Metropolis, 1927; Dystopianism; Expressionism; FX-ism

Mifune, 1999; Dogmetism

Mildred Pierce; 1945; Emotionalism

Milk, 2008; Biographism

The Mirror, 1997; Realism

Missing, 1982; Liberalism

Moana, 1926; Documentarism; Eroticism

Modern Life, 2008; Documentarism

Motion Painting, 1947; Avant-Gardism

Moulin Rouge, 2001; Musicalism

Mr Deeds Goes to Town, 1936; Utopianism

Mr Smith Goes to Washington, 1939; Utopianism

The Mummy, 1932; Horrorism

Munchhausen, 1943; Escapism; Illusionism

Murder My Sweet, 1944; Film Noirism

The Music Box, 1932; Slapstickism

My American Uncle, 1980; Naturalism

My Darling Clementine, 1946; Westernism

My Favorite Wife, 1940; Screwballism

My Man Godfrey, 1936; Screwballism

My Own Private Idaho, 1991; American Indieism

Les mystères du château de Dé, 1929; Avant-Gardism

N

1984, 1956; Dystopianism

Naked, 1993; Realism

Nana, 1926; Naturalism

Nanook of the North, 1922; Documentarism

Napoleon, 1927; Biographism

The New Babylon, 1929; Constructivism

Die Niebelungen (Siegfried and Kriemhild's Revenge), 1924; FX-ism

Night and Fog, 1955; Documentarism

Night of the Living Dead, 1968; American Indieism; Horrorism

North By Northwest, 1959; FX-ism

Nosferatu, 1922; Caligarism; Expressionism

Now Voyager, 1942; Emotionalism

La nuit du carrefour (Night at the Crossroads), 1932; Poetic Realism

O

Oh! What a Lovely War, 1969; Anti-Militarism

Once Upon a Time in the West, 1968; Westernism

One Sings, The Other Doesn't, 1977; Feminism

On the Town, 1949; Musicalism

On the Waterfront, 1954; Classicism

Open Hearts, 2002; Dogmetism

Opus I–IV, 1921–5; Avant-Gardism

Orphée, 1950; Surrealism

Ossessione, 1942; Italian Neo-Realism; Naturalism

Out of the Past, 1947; Film Noirism

The Outsiders, 1983; Teenagism

P

Paisa, 1947; Italian Neo-Realism

Pandora's Box, 1929; Eroticism; Expressionism

Paris Belongs to Us, 1960; New Wavism

The Passion of Joan of Arc, 1928; Auteurism

Paths of Glory, 1957; Anti-Militarism

Patton, 1970; Biographism

Pépé Le Moko, 1936; Poetic Realism

The Perfect Storm, 2000; Disasterism

Persepolis, 2007; Cartoonism

Persona, 1966; Feminism

The Phantom of the Opera, 1925; Horrorism

The Philadelphia Story, 1940; Screwballism

Pink Flamingos, 1972; Cultism

Pinky, 1949; Liberalism

Platform, 2000; Asian Militarism

The Plow That Broke the Plains, 1936; Propagandism

Porky's, 1982; Teenagism

The Poseidon Adventure, 1972; ; Disasterism

Psycho, 1960; Expressionism; Horrorism

The Public Enemy, 1931; Gangsterism

Pulp Fiction, 1994; Gangsterism

Q

Le quai des brumes (Port of Shadows), 1938; Poetic Realism

Quo Vadis?, 1956; Monumentalism

R

Raging Bull, 1980; Athleticism

Raiders of the Lost Ark, 1981; Escapism

Raise the Red Lantern, 1991; Orientalism

Ran, 1985; Auteurism

Ray, 2004; Biographism

Rebel Without a Cause, 1955; Teenagism

Red River, 1948; Westernism

Reefer Madness, 1936; Cultism

La reine Margot, 1994; Costume Romanticism

Repulsion, 1965; Eroticism

Reservoir Dogs, 1982; American Indieism; Gangsterism; Postmodernism

Rhythmus 21, 1921–4; Avant-Gardism

Ride the High Country, 1962; Revisionism

The Ring, 1998; Horrorism

Rio Bravo, 1959; Westernism

Risky Business, 1983; Teenagism

Robin Hood, 1922; Athleticism

The Rocky Horror Picture Show, 1975; Cultism

Romancing the Stone, 1984; Escapism

Rome, Open City, 1945; Italian Neo-Realism

La ronde, 1950; Auteurism

Rosemary's Baby, 1968; Horrorism

The Roundup, 1965; Auteurism

RR, 2008; Experimentalism

The Rules of the Game, 1939; Realism

Run Lola Run, 1998; Postmodernism

S

Safety Last, 1923; Slapstickism

Salo, 1975; Auteurism

Le Samurai, 1967; Gangsterism

San Francisco, 1936; Disasterism

Saturday Night Fever, 1977; Musicalism

Scarface, 1932; Gangsterism

Scarlet Street, 1945; Naturalism

Scorpio Rising, 1964; Experimentalism

The Searchers, 1956; Auteurism; Westernism

Secrets and Lies, 1996; Naturalism

Secrets of a Soul, 1926; Expressionism

The Seven Samurai, 1954; Orientalism

The Seventh Seal, 1957; Auteurism

Shadow of a Doubt, 1943; Utopianism

Shane, 1953; Westernism

Shanghai Express, 1932; Exoticism

Shchors, 1939; Socialist Realism

She Wore a Yellow Ribbon, 1949; Westernism

Shirin, 2008; Minimalism

Shoah, 1985; Documentarism

Shoot the Pianist, 1960; Revisionism

Shrek, 2001; Cartoonism

Sicko, 2007; Liberalism

The Sign of Leo, 1959; New Wavism

Singin' In The Rain, 1952; Hollywood Studioism; Musicalism

Sleep, 1963; Avant-Gardism; Experimentalism; Minimalism

The Smiling Madame Beudet, 1923; Feminism

Snow White and the Seven Dwarfs, 1937; Cartoonism

Song of the South, 1946; Racialism

Songs from the Second Floor, 2000; Surrealism

The Sorrow and the Pity, 1969; Documentarism

Soylent Green, 1973; Dystopianism

Spirited Away; 2001; Cartoonism

Splendor in the Grass, 1961; Teenagism

Spring, Summer, Autumn, Winter … and Spring, 2003; Orientalism

Stagecoach, 1939; Racialism; Westernism

Stalker, 1979; Auteurism

Star Wars, 1977; FX-ism

State Fair; 1933; Utopianism

Steamboat Bill, Jr, 1928; Slapstickism

Steamboat Round The Bend, 1935; Utopianism

Steamboat Willie, 1928; Cartoonism

Stella Dallas, 1937; Emotionalism

Still Life, 2006; Asian Minimalism

Still Walking, 2008; Asian Minimalism

The Story of Louis Pasteur, 1936; Biographism

La Strada, 1954; Italian Neo-Realism

Stranger Than Paradise, 1984; American Indieism; Minimalism

The Strike, 1924; Constructivism

Subway, 1985; Postmodernism

Sunless, 1983; Avant-Gardism

Sweet Sixteen, 2003; Realism

T

13 Lakes, 2004; Experimentalism

2001: A Space Odyssey, 1968; FX-ism

Tabu, 1931; Exoticism

Taxi Driver, 1976; Classicism

Ten, 2002; Feminism; Miminalism

The Ten Commandments; Monumentalism

The Terminator, 1984; Dystopianism

Thelma and Louise, 1991; Feminism

Thérèse Raquin, 1953; Naturalism

The Thief of Bagdad, 1924; Athleticism; Illusionism

The Thin Blue Line, 1988; Documentarism

Things To Come, 1936; Dystopianism

This is Spinal Tap, 1984; Cultism

This Sporting Life, 1963; Naturalism

Three Coins in the Fountain, 1954; Escapism

Three Colours: Blue, 1993, White, Red, 1994 ; Auteurism

The Three Musketeers, 1921; Athleticism

The Three Must-Get-Theirs, 1922; Slapstickism

Three Times, 2006; Asian Minimalism

Through the Olive Trees, 1994; Minimalism

Tie Me Up Tie Me Down, 1990; Eroticism

Time Bandits, 1981; Illusionism

Titanic, 1997; Disasterism

To Kill a Mockingbird, 1963; Liberalism

Tokyo Story, 1953; Orientalism

Top Hat, 1935; Hollywood Studioism

Touch of Evil, 1958; Film Noirism

The Towering Inferno, 1974; Disasterism

Toy Story, 1995; Cartoonism

The Triplets of Belleville, 2003; Cartoonism

A Trip to The Moon (Le voyage dans la lune), 1902; Illusionism

Triumph of the Will, 1935; Propagandism

The True Story of Jesse James, 1957; Biographism

Tropical Malady, 2004; Asian Minimalism

Trouble in Paradise, 1932; Escapism

Twelve Angry Men, 1957; Liberalism

Two-Lane Blacktop, 1971; Cultism

Two Stage Sisters, 1965;   Socialist Realism

U

Ugetsu Monogatari, 1953; Orientalism

Umberto D, 1952;   Italian Neo-Realism

The Umbrellas of Cherbourg, 1964; Escapism; Musicalism

Unconquered, 1947; Racialism

Unforgiven, 1992; Westernism

V

Vampyr, 1932; Horrorism

Venom and Eternity, 1951; Experimentalism

Vertical Ray of the Sun, 2000; Asian Minimalism

Vertigo, 1958; Auteurism

Vivre sa vie (It's My Life), 1962; New Wavism

W

Wall Street, 1987; Liberalism

Waltz with Bashir, 2008; Cartoonism

War and Peace, 1966; Anti-Militarism

Watering the Gardener, 1895; Slapstickism

Wavelength, 1966; Experimentalism

Waxworks, 1924; Caligarism

Way Down East, 1920; Emotionalism

The Werckmeister Harmonies, 2000; Minimalism

Westfront 1918, 1930; Anti-Militarism

West Side Story, 1961; Musicalism

What's Up, Doc?, 1972; Screwballism

White Heat, 1949; Gangsterism

Who Framed Roger Rabbit?, 1988; FX-ism

The Wicked Lady, 1945; Costume Romanticism

The Wicker Man, 1973; Cultism

Wild At Heart, 1990; Postmodernism

The Wild Bunch, 1969; Revisionism; Westernism

Withnail and I, 1987; Cultism

The Wizard of Oz, 1939; Escapism; Illusionism; Utopianism

The Woman From Nowhere (La femme de nulle part); 1922; Avant-Gardism

Woman is the Future of Man, 2004; Asian Minimalism

A Woman Under the Influence, 1974; Naturalism

Women on the Verge of a Nervous Breakdown, 1988; Feminism

Woodstock, 1970; Teenagism

The Wrong Trousers; 1993; Cartoonism

Y

Yankee Doodle Dandy, 1942; Biographism

Yi Yi, 2000; Asian Minimalism

The Young Lady and the Hooligan, 1918; Constructivism

Young Mr Lincoln, 1939; Biographism

Y tu mamá también (And Your Mother Too), 2001; Eroticism

Z

Zoms Lemma, 1970; Experimentalism